SPIRITUAL HEALING
IN A SCIENTIFIC AGE

SPIRITUAL HEALING
IN A SCIENTIFIC AGE

ROBERT PEEL

1817

Harper & Row, Publishers, San Francisco

Cambridge, Hagerstown, New York, Philadelphia, Washington
London, Mexico City, São Paulo, Singapore, Sidney

For permission to reprint copyrighted material, grateful acknowledgment is made to the following: The Christian Science Board of Directors for quotations from Mrs. Eddy's published works; Trustees of The Christian Science Publishing Society for quotations from works published by them; Gerald Duckworth & Co. for passages from Geoffrey Hoyland, *The Resurrection Pattern* © 1947; Yale University Press for a passage from Howard Clark Kee, *Miracle in the Early Christian World* © 1983; Appleton-Century-Crofts for a passage from D. E. Harken in *Cardiac Surgery*, ed. John C. Norman, © 1972; Cambridge University Press for passages from Erwin Schrödinger, *What Is Life?* © 1946, and Werner Heisenberg, *Physics and Beyond* © 1971; Simon and Schuster, Inc. for passages from *Basic Writings of Bertrand Russell*, ed. Egner and Dennon © 1961, Paul Davies, *God and the New Physics* © 1983, and Fritjov Capra, *The Turning Point* © 1982; SCM Press for an extract from Ernst and Marie-Luise Keller, *Miracles in Dispute: A Continuing Debate* © 1969; *The New England Journal of Medicine* for a quotation from David Hilfiker, "Facing Our Mistakes," 1–12–84 and a report by the Massachusetts Department of Public Health, 2–14–74; Scribner's for passages from *The Ante-Nicene Fathers*, eds. Roberts and Donaldson © 1885–96 by Christian Literature Publishing Co., George Santayana, *Interpretations of Poetry and Religion* © 1911, Paul Tillich, *The New Being* © 1955, and Michael Grant, *Jesus: An Historian's Review of the Gospels* © 1977; Paulist Press for a passage from Raymond E. Brown, *New Testament Essays* © 1965, 1982; Harper & Row for a passage from Mark Twain, *Christian Science* © 1907; A. D. Peters & Co. for a quotation from Arthur Koestler, *The Roots of Coincidence* © 1972 by Hutchinson Publishing Group Ltd.; *Boston Globe* for extract from interview with John E. Wennberg by Richard A. Knox, "Surgery or Not?" 8–15–84; *Harvard Magazine* for passages from Derek Bok, "Needed: A new way to train doctors," May-June 1984, and Dava Sobel, "The Hospital Fever," May-June 1978; *British Medical Journal* and Rex Gardner for a passage from "Miracles of healing in Anglo-Celtic Northumbria as recorded by the Venerable Bede and his contemporaries: a reappraisal in the light of twentieth century experience," Dec. 1983; M. L. Firsoff for a passage from Valdemar A. Firsoff, *Life, Mind and Galaxies* © 1967 by Oliver and Boyd; Christian Century Foundation for a passage from Robert Inchausti, "Solzhenitsyn: Postmodern Moralist," *The Christian Century*, 11–14–84 © 1984; Harcourt Brace Jovanovich, Inc. for three lines from T. S. Eliot, "Choruses from the Rock," *Collected Poems 1909–1935* © 1936, renewed 1963, 1964 by T. S. Eliot; Macmillan Publishing Company for four lines from "Two Songs from a Play," *Collected Poems* by William Butler Yeats © 1951, renewed 1956 by Georgie Yeats; and Basic Books for a passage from Steven Weinberg, *The First Three Minutes* © 1977 by Steven Weinberg.

FIRST EDITION

Library of Congress Cataloging-in-Publication Data

Peel, Robert.
  Spiritual healing in a scientific age.

  Bibliography: p.
  1. Spiritual healing. 2. Religion and science—
1946–   . I. Title.
BT732.5.P42 1987   234'.13   86-43015
ISBN 0-06-066484-3

87 88 89 90 91 RRD 10 9 8 7 6 5 4 3 2 1

Contents

Preface

A considerable literature about Christian healing has grown up during the past forty years. Several books, with varying degrees of scholarship, have traced the history of the phenomenon from the first century to the present day. Others have examined the scope, varieties, methods, and claims of spiritual healing in today's world. Still others have approached the subject with an inspirational and instructional purpose, or as an aspect of Christian theology.

Why, then, another book?

Because this profoundly challenging subject cannot be relegated to the fringe of contemporary thought as a mere freak of survival from the past. At present the rocketing materialism of our age threatens Christianity itself with obsolescence. But the same adventurous spirit that has powered this century's scientific and technological triumphs can and must be brought to the fresh exploration of its neglected spiritual resources. And this is equally important for a beleaguered Christianity and an oveerconfident scientism.

In the confrontation between religious and scientific values, Christian healing occupies a possibly unique place. At a point where the two sets of values clearly intersect, the mere existence of such healing as a concrete fact of modern life has startling implications.

At the present time, to be sure, the subject comes up mostly in areas of interest at a safe distance from the mainstream of modern thought, particularly of scientific thought. Also at some distance from the well-groomed but constricted pastures of modernized religious thinking.

It is true that during the past few decades some of the leading Christian denominations have come to recognize the revival of interest in spiritual healing in their own ranks. This limited upsurge has, in general, won their toleration and, in some cases, their admiration or even encouragement. But the trend so far is definitely outside the churches' chief concerns. It is also held back by their obvious anxiety lest so fervent a movement overstep the mark, claim too much, venture too far, and get into serious trouble by contesting the established authority of science in the care and cure of the body.

For that reason the new healing movement as a whole has looked somewhat warily at Christian Science, whose very name suggests a scandalous challenge to both the religion of the past and the science of the present.

In the literature of spiritual healing the references to Christian Science are few and far between. Some of them are cautiously appreciative, some loftily critical, some slightly embarrassed. The present book tries to look more closely at several of the crucial issues raised by the radical commitment of Christian Scientists for more than a hundred years to wholly spiritual methods of healing.

While using this focus to examine neglected aspects of the spiritual healing movement's relation to the secular science and secularized Christianity of our day, the book aims at something far larger than sectarian apologetics. Its purpose is not prescriptive but heuristic. Or, put more plainly, it explores the further reaches of a largely ignored resource of the spiritual life of our age.

I have quoted liberally from other authors, partly to help readers for whom spiritual healing may be an unfamiliar and suspect subject by providing bridges from more familiar areas of thought and vocabulary. On the other hand, the affidavits and letters of testimony in the second part of the book, as well as three or four of the longer documentary quotations in earlier chapters, are included for a different reason: to show how Christian healing that relies wholly on spiritual methods looks from the inside. To get "inside" history through a variety of individual lives is to reorder history, as Solzhenitsyn showed on a grand scale in *The Gulag Archipelago*.[1]

During the past century society has tended to tolerate Christian Science as it learned earlier to tolerate Quaker pacifism. Each is seen as a kind of spiritual luxury for a few odd souls—permissible and perhaps even inspiring as a very minor element in the great cultural mix, but not to be taken seriously as a challenge to the dominant structures of thought in today's technocratic society.

An analogy drawn almost forty years ago by an English Quaker, Geoffrey Hoyland, in a modest but original little book provides a useful reminder of the danger of dismissing any force or pattern of nature as having such limited power that it can safely be pigeonholed as of minor scientific importance. Hoyland discusses spiritual healing as a phenomenon greatly underestimated (when it is even noticed) by contemporary thought in general; and he offers the following analogy:

Magnetism, to the Victorian scientists, appeared to be a force of strictly limited range and capability; if you had asked Faraday, who was doing brilliant pioneer work in this subject just when Queen Victoria was ascending the throne, whether it would ever be possible to lift a five-ton steel armour-plate by means of a magnet he would probably have shaken his head. There are some patterns in Nature which, though they can do a little, appear to be incapable of doing very much—it is a case of "thus far and no further." But Faraday would have been wrong, none the less, for a modern magnetic crane in a steel works can lift fantastic weights. Methods have been developed of concentrating the magnetic field to an extent which would have been regarded as impossible fifty years ago. *It is dangerous, and unscientific, to say of any of the patterns of Nature that they must always be too weak, or too faint, to achieve a certain specified result.* Patterns have a disconcerting habit of suddenly asserting themselves masterfully; the faint footpath over the heath changes overnight into an arterial road.[2]

This quotation may serve as both a parable and a transition to what follows. The first chapter, however, may be skipped or deferred by readers whose interest in the announced subject of the book does not extend to the philosophic framework of modern scientific thinking about the universe. Such readers may well begin with chapter 2 and return to chapter 1 later if their interest in the subject's larger implications has been sufficiently aroused.

Part 1

VIEWPOINTS

A Hard Look
at an Odd Cosmos

We live in a scientific age.

Or do we?

Certainly the multiplying technological "miracles" of our time invite an almost religious awe when measured against the material accomplishments of past centuries. And the awe mounts as we learn almost daily of the even more dazzling possibilities of scientific research and organized human intelligence to be expected of the years ahead of us.

Except, of course, that the most sensational possibility of all is the threatened self-destruction of the entire human race by the very instruments developed by our age's scientific sophistication. That single possibility of total annihilation changes everything.

To be sure, contemporary physics and cosmology have accustomed us in recent years to the widely accepted scientific hypothesis that the universe, which it holds to have originated from ten to twenty billion years ago in the primeval event known as the Big Bang, is destined by the logic of the second law of thermodynamics to inevitably greater disorder. By the same logic, it must gradually, through fifty or sixty billion years of further expansion, disintegrate into an infinitely cold, dark state of nonbeing.

Or, by the alternative theory that there are limits on the expansion of the universe, it may be expected at some point to start recoiling upon itself. Then, the theory goes, by a gradual process of contraction it would be drawn back through all its previous stages until in one last mad rush it would revert to the state of incredibly hot, unimaginably dense energy that is thought to have generated it in the first place.

Today both theories are meeting with increased challenge. But whatever scenario one chooses, our current scientific models of the physical universe reduce the fate of the inhabitants of our small planet to a matter of almost trivial concern. In the stupendous drama of cosmic evolution presented to us by today's mathematical wizards and stargazers, even the anticipated death of the solar system would be only a minor incident. Bertrand Russell summed it all up in a now classic passage:

> That man is the product of causes which had no prevision of the ends they were achieving; that his origin, his growth, his hopes and fears, his loves and his beliefs are but the outcome of accidental collocations of atoms; . . . that all the labours of the ages, all the devotion, all the inspiration, all the noonday brightness of human genius, are destined to extinction in the vast death of the solar system, and that the whole of man's achievement must inevitably be buried beneath the debris of a universe in ruins—all these things, if not quite beyond dispute, are . . . nearly certain. . . . Brief and powerless is man's life; on him and all his race the slow, sure doom falls pitiless and dark. Blind to good and evil, reckless of destruction, omnipotent matter rolls on its relentless way.[1]

In such a framework, the survival of the endangered human species for a few more thousand or hundred thousand years of precarious earth-living or planet-hopping would seem to have little ultimate value. Even the astounding possibilities opened up in this century by relativity, quantum theory, and molecular biology do not challenge in any basic way the flimsy transience of the human enterprise, which the nuclear threat of today brings home even to bright five-year-olds.

It is not surprising that a recurrent strain of melancholy runs through the meditations of many outstanding physical scientists, even as they write with pride of the immense intellectual adventure on which they have jointly embarked. This is illustrated in a reflective comment by a physicist whose competence extends from elementary particle physics to current theory on the genesis of the universe. In a popularized presentation of this latter subject, Nobel prizewinner Steven Weinberg concludes with a passage written in an airplane thirty thousand feet above Wyoming:

> Below, the earth looks very soft and comfortable—fluffy clouds here and there, snow turning pink as the sun sets, roads stretching straight across the country from one town to another. It is very hard to realize that all this is just a tiny part of an overwhelmingly hostile universe. It is even harder to realize that this present universe has evolved from an unspeakably unfamiliar early condition, and faces a future extinction of endless cold or intolerable heat. The more the universe seems comprehensible, the more it also seems pointless.
>
> But if there is no solace in the fruits of our research, there is at least some consolation in the research itself. Men and women are not content to comfort themselves with tales of gods and giants, or to confine their thoughts to the daily affairs of life; they also build tele-scopes and satellites and accelerators, and sit at their desks for endless hours working out the meaning of the data they gather. The effort to understand the universe is one of the very few things that lifts human life a little above the level of farce, and gives it some of the grace of tragedy.[2]

Here speaks one faction of contemporary scientific thought, not without its own stoic beauty and self-enclosed logic. Yes, we do live in a scientific age, it insists, but to be true to that fact we must in the last analysis reduce the human spirit and all its values to the interaction of elementary particles of matter/energy.

Another kind of scientific mentality, with an innate craving for ultimate meaning, substitutes a rapturous cosmic mysticism for the traditional theologies it finds unacceptable. This mysticism, in its various forms, stands in reverential awe before the beauty and wonder, the mathematical order, the marvelous complexity and, it hopes, the underlying simplicity of the universe progressively being revealed to scientific research and speculation.

In this great unfolding pageant it finds the evidence or at least the possibility of a cosmic mind or consciousness governing or inhering in everything from the most evanescent sub-atomic particle to the universe in its indecipherable totality. The term *God* is considered by some to be reasonably acceptable to designate this mind—but God the great impersonal mathematician, not God the loving Father of Christian faith.

As with all forms of pantheism or panpsychism, this scientific vision holds no promise of release from the colossal waste, cruelty, disaster, and final dissolution of its deified physical universe. It is open to the same kind of humanistic criticism that George Santayana offered about Emerson's cosmic optimism—an optimism not unrelated to Einstein's religious awe at "the beauty of the logical simplicity" in the order and harmony of the physical universe. As Santayana ironically described this point of view:

> There is evil, of course, [in the human life permitted by such a cosmos]. Experience is sad. There is a crack in everything that God has made. But, ah! the laws of the universe are sacred and beneficent. Without them nothing good could arise. All things, then, are in their right places and the universe is perfect above our querulous tears. Perfect? we may ask. But perfect from what point of view, in reference to what ideal? To its own? To that of a man who renouncing himself and all naturally dear to him, ignoring the injustice, suffering, and impotence in the world, allows his will and his conscience to be hypnotized by the spectacle of a necessary evolution, and lulled into cruelty by the pomp and music of a tragic show? In that case the evil is not explained, it is forgotten; it is not cured, but condoned.[3]

With the word *cured* we reach at last the real subject of this book. To cure is to change the evidence before the human senses, to actualize the possibility of a good that transcends but also transforms a disordered situation. The disorder may be a malfunctioning bodily organ or a physical universe emptied of ultimate meaning—emptied, for millions of people today, of a believably loving and all-powerful God.

Questions of cosmology may seem far removed from the question of Christian healing, but in fact they are intimately and intricately interrelated. The old Newtonian clockwork universe of mechanical cause and effect left no room for accepting the New Testament accounts of healing as actual or possible. To escape that dilemma, most Christians in the three centuries intellectually dominated by classical Newtonian science were driven to posit a God who for his own inscrutable purpose set aside every now and then the immutable and inviolable laws of nature, which he himself had established for the supposed benefit of his whole creation.

The new physics of this century has changed the Newtonian picture almost beyond recognition. It has penetrated to the heart of the atom and found there the principle of uncertainty. It has looked up at the heavens, at space and time, and found them to be not the work of God's hands but the construction of mortals' limited modes of perception. Each successive theoretical model of the universe put forward in this century has given new (and wry) meaning to the psalmist's words on the wonders of the cosmos: "Yea, all of them shall wax old like a garment; as a vesture shalt thou change them, and they shall be changed"[4] (Ps. 102:26, KJV).

The crucial change in the scientific revolution of this century is the breaking down of the long-held assumption that absolutely pure scientific objectivity is possible. More and more, the scientist is seen as a participant in nature's processes, not merely an observer.

In quantum mechanics the act of observation is an integral part of the event being observed. But there are many other kinds of involvement. For instance, the development of nuclear theory has led to the practical possibility of global holocaust. In the same way, elementary particle physics (with a nod to relativity theory) has led to the actuality of space travel and therefore the possibility of space war.

Even in the new biology, which lags behind physics in challenging the materialistic determinism of the past, the basic concepts of evolution and adaptation have opened the way for redirecting the evolutionary process through genetic engineering with its radical consequences for medicine, industry, agriculture. And, of course, it also holds incalculable potential for some fatal interference with the genetic balance of humankind through runaway biogenetic experimentation, not to mention the ravages of bacterial warfare.

When the first atomic bomb went off in the New Mexico desert, the watching scientists who had worked on it so long and devotedly almost danced with joy at the successful completion of their incredibly demanding task. Only J. Robert Oppenheimer, who had brilliantly piloted the project through all its difficulties, stood apart. With stunned realization as the mushroom cloud expanded, he repeated the fateful words of the Bhagavad Gita: "I am become death, the destroyer of worlds." It was a moment that marked a new era in scientific sensibility.

Stated less apocalyptically, the quantitative measurements of science and the qualitative judgments of ethics and religion can no longer be kept in two entirely separate categories. It becomes possible to ask whether the scientific spirit can logically rule out a priori the possibility of a "spiritual" healing force. A force, that is to say, lying well beyond quantification and analysis by the present instruments and techniques of human invention but pragmatically observable and qualitatively measurable in its effects on human experience.

However, the word *spiritual* is meaningless to many natural scientists today. Others may equate it loosely with cultural values of strictly human origin. To regard spirit or mind—let alone the Holy Spirit or Divine Mind—as an entity or power operating through higher laws to overrule and alter the perceived mechanism of the physical universe is therefore to invite instant dismissal by a large part of the scientific community. "Where is your evidence?" they quite naturally ask, and often with considerable scorn. That is the question to which the rest of this book addresses itself.

CHAPTER 2

A Traveler from Inner Space

Science fiction has acquainted us with travelers from outer space who bring with them extraterrestrial wisdom and skills beyond the grasp of a human race shaped by its own limited experience.

According to the records we have, Jesus of Nazareth could well have appeared to his contemporaries to be just such a figure. Except that he might be better described as a traveler from inner space—from a world of thought completely transcending the limits of the space-time universe we know.

In his own reported words, he was "sent" by "the Father"— his intimate name for a God who was Truth itself—to reveal a new order of being, a new reality, a new relationship between divinity and humanity. New, that is, to earthbound mentalities.

Drawing his language from the religious culture of the time and place to which he addressed himself, Jesus described this new state of being as "the kingdom of God" or "the kingdom of heaven." This kingdom, he told his wondering listeners, is "within you" (Luke 17:21). It is not merely a postmortem reward or otherworldly alternative to mortal existence, but an immediately operative power in the lives of those who receive it into their hearts and minds.

He accompanied his words with what seemed to the public a series of supernatural happenings or miracles, though to Jesus they were obviously the perfectly natural signs or evidence of the transforming power of the reality he was presenting to the world. He clearly expected that his followers, too, would provide the same sort of evidence. "He that believeth on me," he announced, "the works that I do shall he do also" (John 14:12). Half promise, half command, his words set no time limit on the ministry of healing, which remains profoundly rooted in the primitive Christian gospel.

This, of course, raises at once the question of the historicity of the words and events recorded in the New Testament. But before addressing that question, it may be useful to take a deeper look at the significance that the biblical accounts assign to the healings.

In the first place, such spiritual or divine healing was taken for granted by the first Christians as an essential part of the coming of "the kingdom." More than a mere humanitarian rescue, it bore witness to a God of infinite love as well as infinite power. This image of God stood in welcome contrast to the prevalent concept of a punitive deity visiting his wrath upon a race of sinners whom he himself (presumably knowing what the outcome would be) had created vulnerable to the deceptive blandishments of sin in all its forms.

In the world of spiritual values from which Jesus spoke and acted, the First Cause was Love itself, embracing in its infinitely compassionate care the whole of its creation. But how could anyone seriously believe in such a governing power, in the face of all the failure, pain, and grief mixed in with the temporal triumphs of the human spirit?

The answer of Jesus was not an argument but a life, as many writers have pointed out. What is not so generally recognized is the crucial part healing played in that remarkable life. One writer in this century describes it as a new "mode of speech," more effective than words in reaching minds enslaved by material appearances. It was telling them of a spiritual reality ready to transform their broken and meager lives, and it spoke to them with a vivid authority unknown to their own religious teachers. The same writer, relating the healings of Jesus to John's great affirmation that "the Word was made flesh, and dwelt among us . . . full of grace and truth" (John 1:14), goes on to say:

> Contrast this with the method of philosophy, its dialectic, its detachment from the human need. Set philosophy beside the actual healing of the palsied man, the blind, the lame. The infinite breaks into a new kind of utterance, speaking the language comprehensible to men.[1]

Seen in this light, Jesus the Christ is far more than a wonder-worker or primitive psychotherapist. In its largest terms, his ultimate purpose stands out as the healing of humanity's alienation from God, a cosmic task that included the overcoming of sin, death, finitude itself—but also of sickness, bodily disability, and mental disorder built into the physically perceived world as another form of entropy.

So central was his healing work to his mission that Jesus could remark to those who doubted his message, "If I do not the works of my Father, believe me not. But if I do, though ye believe not me, believe the works" (John 10:37, 38).

The skeptics of his own day had an easy answer for that one. They could hardly deny the works, which were palpably evident, but they attributed them not to divine power but to Beelzebub, the prince of the devils. So much for believing in Jesus as the emissary of God!

Christians of this age have had a harder time with the question. Biblical scholarship for 150 years since David Friedrich Strauss's epoch-making *Life of Jesus* has tended increasingly to regard the miracles of the New Testament as either myths or factual events embroidered with mythical elements. As Spinoza, Strauss, Ludwig Andreas Feuerbach, Joseph Ernest Renan, and Albert Schweitzer have done for earlier periods, so Rudolph Bultmann (for all the depth dimension of his religious thinking) has carried the demythologizing process further along for a whole generation of modernist theologians.[2]

Nevertheless, a quiet countercurrent has set in among practicing Christians in our time. By the middle of the century, even a theologian so deeply involved in the critical culture of his day as Paul Tillich could answer his own question "How do we paint Jesus the Christ?" by pointing to the gospel stories that present the historical Jesus as healer no less than Savior. Tillich went on to say:

It is astonishing that this color, this vivid expression of His nature, this powerful trait of His character, has more and more been lost in our time. The grayish colors of a moral teacher, the tense expression of a social reformer, the soft traits of a suffering servant have prevailed, at least amongst our painters and theologians and life-of-Jesus novelists; perhaps not so much in the hearts of the people who need somebody to heal them.

The gospels, certainly, are not responsible for this disappearance of power in the picture of Jesus. They abound in stories of healing; but *we* are responsible, ministers, laymen, theologians, who forgot that "Savior" means "healer," he who makes whole and sane what is broken and insane, in body and mind. . . .

Are we still able to experience this power? . . . Of course we were worried about miracle-stories for many decades; today we know what the New Testament always knew—that miracles are signs pointing to the presence of a divine power in nature and history, and that they are in no way negations of natural laws.[3]

The last clause in the last sentence is questionable. But it helps to explain why Tillich himself never actually engaged in the healing ministry and why he shied away from any form it might take or commitment it might demand that could be regarded as intellectually disreputable. The challenge to "natural laws" is the crux of the whole question of Christian healing.

The "miracles" of Jesus do not make logical sense to those who take natural laws to be divine ordinances. But these "laws" can also be understood as the best provisional formulations the human intellect can offer, at any given stage of development, of how—though not why—nature works as it does. Only if such miracles are hypothesized as the natural result of higher laws that lie beyond the conceptual or verifiable reach of present scientific methodologies can the demands of conventional logic and Christian revelation be reconciled. But only the rare natural scientist is willing as yet to consider this a possibility.

The New Testament makes clear that to the apostles who carried through the Mediterranean world the gospel or good news of the coming of "the kingdom," healing was as natural as the moral and spiritual redemption to which it was closely allied. From their Master they had learned that healing, like salvation, was the work of God's grace, not human skill. Jesus himself had told them, "I can of mine own self do nothing: . . . the Father that dwelleth in me, he doeth the works" (John 5:30, 14:10).

In the minds of his early followers there was clearly nothing magical or esoteric about it. Healing was simply an integral part of the new order brought into effect by the Son of God who, as Paul wrote to young Timothy, "hath abolished death, and hath brought life and immortality to light through the gospel" (2 Tim. 1:10).

But in quoting those words, one encounters again the question of historicity. Modern scholarship raises strong doubts that Paul was the author of this letter to Timothy. How can one base solid conclusions on such uncertain sources? How can one be sure that the healings reported in the New Testament really took place? How indeed can one be certain that Jesus of Nazareth ever existed?

These questions and others like them have been argued pro and con in thousands of volumes. The further one digs into this literature, the clearer it becomes that scholarship and intellectual analysis will never of themselves furnish definitive answers to most of the questions. For instance, scientific humanists who cannot admit the reality of a spiritual power that is neither detectable nor measurable by their instruments are bound to dismiss the New Testament healings as either baseless legend or grossly exaggerated cures of psychosomatic ills rooted in emotional disorders.

On the other hand, true believers are apt to fall back in the end on their simple faith in the person and power of Jesus. There are many persuasive arguments, both historical and rational, for the basic historicity of the New Testament, but traditional Christianity has generally put the highest value on unquestioning faith. In its most evangelical and simplified form this is well illustrated by Billy Graham's statement that even if "there were no historical record of Jesus' life and ministry, He would still be real to me because I know Him by personal and daily experience."[4]

With the revival of spiritual healing in our own scientific age, however, a resource has been restored that has been missing as a widespread phenomenon since the first few centuries of the Christian era. This is the actual *experiencing* in one's own life of the same sorts of healings recorded in the Gospels.

When an overnight healing of terminal cancer, at the very point where death seems imminent, takes place through the prayer of a Christian healer called in at the last moment (see p. 186), it is not difficult for the one who has had the healing to accept the possibility of Jesus' instantaneous cure of a man "full of leprosy" or another "born blind" (Luke 5:12, 13; John 9:1–32).

Or when a woman who has had a long medical history of hospitalization, with batteries of medical specialists, tests, and treatments, and with complications of Ménière's disease, thyroid trouble, blood clotting, and a cardiac condition for which a coronary bypass operation has been prescribed, is finally and completely healed through three days' study of Christian Science (see pp. 69–73), she will obviously find quite understandable the spiritual healing in Galilee two thousand years ago of a "certain woman, which had an issue of blood twelve years, and had suffered many things of many physicians, and had spent all that she had, and was nothing bettered, but rather grew worse" (Mark 5:25, 26).

In the past few decades there have been a number of serious, scholarly studies of the recorded healings of Jesus and his followers during the early centuries of Christianity. Especially notable are Evelyn Frost's pioneer work *Christian Healing* and Morton T. Kelsey's *Healing and Christianity.* The latter carries the examination of the evidence of continued healing down to the present day, with a few unfortunate omissions of significant modern areas of such healing, but the chief value of the book lies in its treatment of the subject during the first five hundred years of Christian history.[5]

What emerges from this examination is the naturalness of spiritual healing to the earliest Christians. Sickness, like sin, was the work of Satan, not of the God revealed through Christ Jesus, and both sickness and sin were expected to yield to the prayer of faith. But as Christianity through mass conversions and accelerated acculturation took on more of the world's materialism, healing through prayer became increasingly a specialized function, confined largely to the priesthood and associated first of all with the sacraments and later with the relics of saints.

As superstition grew, so also did skepticism. Toward the end of the fourth century Augustine rejected both the value and the validity of the healing gift at that time. However, by the year 424 his attitude had changed drastically, and the explanation of this reversal followed two years later in his great work *The City of God*:

I realized how many miracles were occurring in our own day . . . which were so like the miracles of old and also how wrong it would be to allow the memory of these marvels of divine power to perish from among our people. It is only two years ago that the keeping of records was begun here in Hippo, and already, at this writing, we have nearly seventy attested miracles.[6]

More than fifteen hundred and fifty years later, Augustine's reappraisal of spiritual healing would be matched by an article in the *British Medical Journal* discussing seventh-century cases of healing in Anglo-Celtic Northumbria. The author was Dr. Rex Gardner, a British obstetrician and gynecologist who has looked carefully into the wave of charismatic healing which, starting with the Pentecostals, swept through the traditional churches in the last two decades.[7]

With unusual precision Gardner matches case studies drawn from this research with parallel seventh-century healings by Saint Cuthbert, as recorded by the Venerable Bede in his *Vita S. Cuthberti*. These early healings have usually been brushed aside as miracle stories in the hagiographical tradition, despite Bede's otherwise respected stature today as a historian, plus his own claim to have written "in accordance with the principles of true history" and his checking the facts with Cuthbert's community while at least five witnesses of the healings were still alive. But as Gardner points out, the parallel contemporary cases that have been open to medical observation and investigation add a new factor of probability that makes it more difficult to dismiss the seventh-century healings casually as mere fables.

On the other hand, as Gardner admits, it is virtually impossible to prove any so-called miraculous healing, no matter how concrete the evidence, since medical skeptics can always write it off as a case of inexplicable "spontaneous remission." The modern scholar, he points out,

is above believing in miracles, in fact from his view point "scholarship" and "belief in miracles" are mutually exclusive terms. It is therefore understandable that in a study of Anglo-Saxon medicine Bonser has described faith healing as "that dangerous field, placed between theology and medicine, that no one has dared thoroughly to explore." It seems to me that such an exploration is timely. Bonser's use of the words "risk" and "dared," however, proved to be significant.[8]

The risk for the scholar, Gardner adds wryly, is that of academic suicide. Which tells a lot in a little.

One of the problems is with the expressions *faith healing* and *miracle*. Neither is in the vocabulary of many who practice Christian healing wholeheartedly. A typical caveat is that of a Presbyterian chaplain in a large Roman Catholic hospital:

> *Spiritual healing does not involve a suspension of God's laws.* I do not like to hear spiritual healing equated with "miracles." This puts such healing in the realm of the extraordinary and supernatural. When the "wireless" was invented, people called it a miracle. It wasn't; the early radios were merely an application of new knowledge about radio waves which had been in existence, although untapped, from the creation. Similarly, effective prayer for healing taps into the existing spiritual world which is part of the natural order of things. . . . Jesus demonstrated in His ministry an unreserved submission to the divine order which issued forth in His healing power. Thus we must begin a study of the laws governing healing with close scrutiny of Jesus' life and ministry.[9]

It is obvious from both logic and experience that blind faith is not enough. There are many kinds of faith: faith in the doctor or the medicine, faith in a personal charismatic healer, faith in a particular mental technique or in one's own psychic power, faith in a placebo, faith in a God who is presumed on occasion to set aside laws of nature which he himself has ordained; faith in a God who is infinite Love acting through immutable spiritual law.

Any one of these may contribute to a healing, as experience abundantly shows, but only the last can aspire to become more than a blind or somewhat random force. Furthermore, when one dares to speak of a divine order or system of law higher than any attainable by empirical observation, experiment, analysis, and reasoning, this calls for a new order of spiritual understanding, commitment, and practical demonstration of one's faith in one's life.

Two contrasting incidents illustrate what this may mean in relation to Christian healing.

Some years ago a good deal of credence was given to the account of a remarkable healing of cancer experienced by Alice Newton of Leavenworth, Kansas. As recounted by Dr. Rebecca Beard, a physician who was also interested in faith healing,

Newton presented herself to Dr. Beard's little prayer group in St. Louis, asking for help. The cancer was already at a very advanced stage:

> Her appearance when we first saw her shocked us. Her huge abdomen was larger than a woman at full-term pregnancy. She had the dreaded cachexia. Her emaciated body was scarcely able to carry the great burden. Her question was, "Do you think that I can be healed with prayer and nothing else?" For just a moment I felt a sinking feeling. "This is it," I thought.[10]

The request was accepted, however, and Newton returned to her home city with new confidence, saying, "I have absolute faith now that our prayer will be answered, and the Lord will heal me." Two years of prayer followed. Sometimes the faith of Dr. Beard's group faltered a little, but it was always restored and strengthened by the letters they received from Alice Newton, radiant with certainty that the healing would come. Finally came a night when she went to bed about midnight, with no special mental or spiritual preparation. Dr. Beard recounted what followed.

> As she slept she had a vision of the disciples asleep as Jesus came down the mountainside from his lone vigil of prayer. His face was full of sorrow as He looked at the sleeping men, then He glanced over and smiled at her. Immediately the scene changed. It was the day of the crucifixion. The cross was being lowered into the hole that had been dug for it, the Master's body already nailed upon it. Torn with the thought of how the jar would hurt Him, she cried out, "O my Jesus," putting up her hand to steady His body and ease the suffering. At that moment her hand dropped to her abdomen and she awoke.

The abdomen was completely flat. There was no pain. The huge accumulation was gone. She felt all around her, but the bed was dry. It was now three in the morning. The local doctor, a close friend of hers, was summoned. When he arrived expecting an emergency, he was stunned by what he found:

> His questions came short and fast in his excitement. "What passed?" "What came away?" "Was there water?" "Was there blood?" "Did you perspire heavily?" "What was it?" To all she answered truthfully, "Nothing." Finally his questions ceased, for her answers continued to be, "No, nothing passed—nothing came away." At last he said quietly, "No one but God could perform a miracle like that."

For all of them it was just that—a miracle, a setting aside of natural law as generally understood, especially when they found that Newton had lost thirty-eight and a half pounds in that one night's experience. This bulky mass of matter, which had simply disappeared, would have been enough—if it had been transformed into energy as physics would say it must have been—to leave the city of Leavenworth in ruins. For years afterwards, the Leavenworth newspaper and the *Kansas City Star* mentioned this inexplicable happening every January on the anniversary of Newton's healing. When she later had a full physical examination in St. Louis by Dr. Beard, the latter found "every organ fresh and virginal as though [Newton] had never been ill."

It was an experience full of beauty and wonder, but there is no evidence that any of those involved in it went on afterwards to conduct a passionate search for answers to such questions as: What did the disappearance of that thirty-eight and a half pounds show about the nature of matter? If God could choose to bring about such a healing, why did he permit the disease to develop in the first place? What kind of *law* may be involved in such a healing? How does this relate to faith in medical means? How does it relate to Jesus' announcement of the kingdom of God within? What are the implications of such a healing for our very concept of reality?

However, just such questions as these had been asked back in 1866 by a woman in Lynn, Massachusetts, who experienced a healing less dramatic in character than Newton's but vastly more far-reaching in its effect.

On February 3 of that year the *Lynn Reporter* carried a news item to the effect that Mrs. Mary Patterson (now known to the world as Mary Baker Eddy) had been "severely injured" by a fall on the ice a day and a half before. It also reported that Dr. Alvin Cushing, a popular Lynn surgeon and homeopathic doctor, had found her injuries to be internal "and of a very serious nature, inducing spasms and internal suffering," and that she had now been removed to her home in the adjacent village of Swampscott "though in a very critical condition." Her husband, who was away on a business trip, was summoned back by telegraph, and her friends (according to later affidavits or reminiscences by several of them) were told that she had taken the last step she ever would.

Although the nature and extent of her injury remain unclear,[11] it was sufficiently severe for a messenger on the second day to be sent several miles over the icy roads in subzero weather to inform her minister of the accident and warn him of her critical state. More significant, however, is what happened on the third day. Lying in bed helpless and in pain, she read in her Bible the account of one of Jesus' healings. As she read, a flood of light poured into her thought, a sudden insight (as it seemed to her) into the heart of true being. Put in terms closer to her own, it was a revelation of the spiritual perfection of the universe as it exists in the mind of God—or, to use her later terminology, the Mind that *is* God. It was, in short, a new view of reality, to be recognized at the same time as the very kingdom of God preached and practiced by Jesus, the kingdom within made manifest in the outward form of healing.

As this dawned on her, Mrs. Patterson (Eddy) rose from her bed completely healed. Her friends were quick to hail her startling recovery as a miracle, but she herself saw it as the result of divine law. Some years later she summed up in a single sentence what for her was the real miracle: "That short experience included a glimpse of the great fact that I have since tried to make plain to others, namely, Life in and of Spirit; this Life being the sole reality of existence."[12]

The *sole* reality. Here is the essential point that would distinguish the practice of Christian Science from other forms of Christian healing—and also from some of Mrs. Eddy's own earlier experiments in mental and spiritual healing. It would take a good deal more time, thought, study, and experience before she would feel that she had arrived at a full understanding of what she had glimpsed in 1866. Yet Christian healing, she was sure, must rest on more than isolated moments of exalted inspiration—or blind faith—if it were to survive in an age of science. It must rest on both understanding and demonstration. It must partake of the nature of scientific discovery as well as Christian revelation.

It was in this framework that she came to see the 1866 experience as the decisive moment of discovery in her own relation to Christian healing. Later she would write in her book *Science and Health with Key to the Scriptures:*

For three years after my discovery, I sought the solution of this problem of Mind-healing, searched the Scriptures and read little else, kept aloof from society, and devoted time and energies to discovering a positive rule. . . . I knew the Principle of all harmonious Mind-action to be God, and that cures were produced in primitive Christian healing by holy, uplifting faith; but I must know the Science of this healing, and I won my way to absolute conclusions through divine revelation, reason, and demonstration.[13]

This was daring talk for a relatively unknown middle-aged woman in a nineteenth-century American society brimming with material energy, social Darwinism, and male chauvinism, a society backed up by an embattled Christian establishment that considered any talk of reviving apostolic spiritual healing to be nonsensical if not blasphemous. It was also the statement of a pioneer who would organize a religious movement that by its centennial year of 1966 would have built up a record of spiritual healing that is certainly unsurpassed—even if frequently ignored—in the modern world.

Balancing this picture of an untrained woman who could write with all the assurance of any male scientist of the time, certain that he has made a discovery of vast future importance to the world, is another statement about herself that she retained in *Science and Health* through all its later revisions and editions: "To-day, though rejoicing in some progress, she [the author] still finds herself a willing disciple at the heavenly gate, waiting for the Mind of Christ."[14]

In that spirit, both Christian Scientists and traditional Christians can afford to look beyond denominational differences to their common heritage and common purpose in bringing the healing power of Christ to bear on the ills of our present world.

CHAPTER 3

Healing the Sick: Science or Art?

At the end of her partly autobiographical work, *Retrospection and Introspection*, Mary Baker Eddy wrote in 1892:

> I am persuaded that only by the modesty and distinguishing affection illustrated in Jesus' career, can Christian Scientists aid the establishment of Christ's kingdom on the earth. In the first century of the Christian era Jesus' teachings bore much fruit, and the Father was glorified therein. In this period and the forthcoming centuries, watered by dews of divine Science, this "tree of life" will blossom into greater freedom, and its leaves will be "for the healing of the nations."[1]

The phrase "divine Science" in such a context might well raise the hackles of any tough-minded natural scientist who denies the name *science* even to aspects of current cosmological theory which, although they are widely accepted by the scientific community on logical grounds, are not yet precisely measurable or empirically verifiable.[2]

Historically, of course, the word *science* has had many wider uses relating to logic, order, law, and universality. It was traditionally used by the church fathers and medieval schoolmen as a metaphysical term. *"Perfecta scientia Deum scire"* (Perfect science is the knowledge of God), St. Hilary declared in the fourth century. Even the modern scientist can tolerate such an assertion as the quaint product of an age of religious dogmatism and scientific ignorance. By the time of Thomas Aquinas, theology as "science" had split amoebalike into two branches, Divine Science and Science of God, differentiated by minute philosophic distinctions. But today such usage inevitably invites the wrath of those natural scientists who see it as poaching on their own ground. Consequently, most advocates of Christian healing are quick to disclaim any scientific aspirations and to accept a collaborative or clearly subordinate role in relation to medical science.

The question whether medicine is a science or an art—or both—has been argued for many years. Until recently many doctors, especially older general practitioners, have both practiced and regarded it in large measure as an art. But in the past few decades the development that began with the miracle drugs of the midcentury and proliferated magically to the *in vitro* fertilization and recombinant DNA techniques of today has brought a widespread conviction that biomedicine, even if a late arrival, is at last a bona fide science.[3]

Yet the development has also brought its own embarrassments. It has not abolished human fallibility in medical practice and administration. In America it has raised expectations in the general populace beyond all reason, with a resulting flood of malpractice suits against conscientious doctors and over-burdened institutions because they cannot always deliver the results anticipated. It has lost sight of the whole person in its development of narrow specialists. It has produced a public almost pathologically concerned with health and abjectly reliant on drugs. At the same time it has produced a stupendous research and health care industry, eating up incredible billions of dollars every year. Significantly its Washington lobby is second in power only to the arms industry that provides us with our apocalyptic engines of death.

Today's biomedicine rests philosophically on the concept of the human being as a physical organism shaped in the last analysis by the interaction of chance and law through eons of cosmic, molecular, geological, and finally biological development. Most professing Christians, including Christian doctors, would add to that description their own personal faith in a divine purpose somehow or other at work through this long evolutionary process. But the fact remains that medicine *as a putative natural science* must treat the body as a wholly material phenomenon.

By the strict standards of the "hard" physical sciences, the scientific doctor is the specialist who treats a particular disease, not the general practitioner who may to some extent minister to the whole person. The latter may take into account psychological, social, moral, or even spiritual factors far more important to healing in a given instance than the biochemical expertise of specialists treating the affected organs or functions as somewhat autonomous though closely interrelated parts of a complex material mechanism. Yet the specialists tend to have the final say in our technological society, with computerized medicine on hand to produce its statistical data, make its lightning diagnoses, and deliver its mechanical judgments—in the doctor's office, the clinic, the operating room, the emergency room, the intensive care unit.

The medical triumphs of this century are generally regarded as among the wonders of our age. Less well known is the extensive, documented literature challenging modern medicine's right to be accounted an exact science or even a socially satisfactory system of health care. This dissatisfaction is by no means confined to such crusading critics as Ivan Illich and Robert S. Mendelsohn, with their insistence that medical science still causes as many diseases as it cures.[4] The criticisms extend through hundreds of sober medical reports, sociological studies, ethical disquisitions, economic analyses, legal decisions, popular magazine articles, and academic investigations. As President Derek Bok of Harvard ruefully suggested in a carefully balanced 1983 report on the needs of the university's medical school, "Dean Burwell was only partly facetious in stating to Harvard medical students: 'Half of what we have taught you is wrong. Unfortunately we do not know which half.' "[5]

This book is not intended to belittle a profession so distinguished by dedicated zeal as the physician's. Even a Christian Scientist is not likely to forget the words of Science and Health: "It is just to say that generally the cultured class of medical practitioners are grand men and women, therefore they are more scientific than are false claimants to Christian Science"[6]—and of its author's further statement in regard to such false claimants: "I should have more faith in an honest drugging-doctor, one who abides by his statements and works upon as high a basis as he understands, healing me, than I could or would have in a smooth-tongued hypocrite or mental malpractitioner."[7]

Nor in detailing some of the limitations of medicine today do I intend to deny or belittle its manifest successes. For that reason I have drawn my examples almost entirely from the self-critical medical literature already referred to, with deep appreciation of the honesty and the humane as well as scientific concern it illustrates.

We can now look at some of the human errors that may give pause to the medical establishment's claim to sole authority in questions of healing.

In the first place, there are the well-known iatrogenic diseases and disasters that bedevil medical practice: the misdiagnoses leading to wrong treatment (sometimes fatal); the needless operations (admittedly huge in number); the careless mistakes in operations (wrong leg amputated, for example); the irresistible desire to experiment with an untried method; the unsuspected allergy of a patient to a prescribed remedy; the dangerous side effects of an endless variety of drugs (frequently advertised, sold, and administered without sufficient warning and all too often without sufficient testing); the more resistant strains of bacteria developed through the long use of antibiotics; the diseases induced by antitoxins; the confusion of the temporary placebo effect of a new drug with a supposed curative value attributed to it.

These are not merely occasional and easily rectifiable errors, nor do they even begin to suggest the magnitude of the risks involved. For instance, nosocomial illness—an umbrella term for a whole catalogue of infections acquired inside the hospital—has proved fatal to some patients who entered the hospital for treatment of a very minor ailment. It was estimated in 1978 that of "32 million persons admitted to American hospitals each year, about 1.5 million develop some kind of nosocomial infection, and 15,000 die of it."[8] This is one of the many reasons that the most conscientious doctors are slow to say that if a person who has died under some other form of treatment had only been brought to a hospital for skilled biomedical or surgical attention, he or she could almost certainly have been saved. The possibilities for error in a clinic or hospital are incomparably greater than, for instance, in a physics laboratory.

An enthusiastic cardiac surgeon, D. E. Harken, lists a few of the drawbacks of the increased automation of monitoring and therapeutic devices:

The complicated but life-saving science fiction world of Intensive

Care Units has produced a series of diseases of and in itself. There have been *psychologic* disadvantages including fear, insomnia and the disturbance of diurnal and circadian rhythms. There have been *mechanical* disadvantages stemming from the improper use of respirators, endotracheal tubes and other equipment. There have been *electrical* hazards varying from simple arrhythmias to burns and electrocution while utilizing otherwise life-saving equipment. There have been *chemical* and bacteriologic or *infectious* accidents due to inappropriate patient segregation or incomplete device precautions in the Intensive Care and Coronary Care Units. Finally, *human factors* have included errors in maintenance, use, interpretation and trauma. This new breed of diseases can hardly be called iatrogenic for they are not primarily caused by the doctor. They are not nosocomial or those caused by the house. They are caused by the things immediately about the patient, so for this new disease form a new word has been created: *periontogenic* diseases. Periontogenic describes those diseases the *"genesis"* of which are in "the things about." These diseases will be corrected when they are recognized only to be replaced by new periontogenic diseases as new monitoring and therapeutic equipment is devised.[9]

Such considerations are sobering. "Despite the progress in medical science and technology," President Bok wrote in his Harvard report, "many studies have revealed that doctors make a disturbing number of major diagnostic errors," and he illustrates this by "a recent survey of 100 autopsies at a prominent teaching hospital" which disclosed such mistakes in twenty-two percent of the cases.[10]

Another area of fallibility is illustrated in a recent study by a Dartmouth Medical School physician, John E. Wennberg, of differences in surgical rates among communities in fairly close proximity, in this case in Massachusetts. Here are a few random statistics from this particular study:

· Framingham, Fitchburg, Attleboro, Holliston had tonsillectomy rates more than two hundred percent above the statewide average.
· People in Hingham are four times as likely as those in Holyoke to have gallbladders removed.
· In some communities nearly half of the births (forty-eight percent) are by Caesarean.
· Holyoke residents had an overall surgical rate nearly one-third higher than the state average.

These disparities obviously do not arise from differences

among the communities but in physician "practice styles." Such small-area studies, Dr. Wennberg declares, "reveal the intellectual confusion and chaos that sits at the root of much medical practice." He concludes, "Most people assume that there is much more science in medicine than there is."[11]

A final quotation from the Bok report brings to this central issue a measured judgment that carries more weight than the impassioned polemics of a Robert Mendelsohn at war with his own profession's claim to scientific authority. For all its academic reserve, the report delivers a quiet wallop:

Fewer doctors are now inclined to think of themselves as simply arriving at logically determined conclusions by applying scientifically tested truths to experimentally derived data. The world today seems much more complicated. Doctors are constantly forced to make educated guesses based on imperfect information. Diseases often have multiple causes, not all of them scientific in nature. The information physicians receive, the symptoms they observe, the outcome of the treatments they prescribe, can all be affected by the ways in which they act and interact with patients. The decisions they make are limited not only by gaps in biological knowledge but by bureaucratic rules and economic pressures. In short, the doctor's world cannot be restricted to science or neatly divided between the known and the unknown. Considerations of many kinds are often jumbled together to form a picture full of uncertainties, requiring the most delicate kinds of judgments and intuitions.[12]

Uncertainties of all kinds! There are uncertainties that are merely temporary gaps in knowledge, and there is the inescapable principle of uncertainty built into our knowledge of the interacting elementary particles theoretically constituting the atom and replacing it as the primal building block of the material universe.

Some physicians believe that the uncertainties of present-day medicine can be cured by a more profound knowledge of biology, the science that underlies today's chemotherapy. But with all the brilliance of its achievements, the molecular biology of our age lags behind quantum physics in recognizing the inherent limits of its own possible knowledge. It is conceivable—indeed, to the Christian it should surely be regarded as inevitable—that in seeking to find the ultimate source of human intelligence in the electrochemistry of the brain and the basic determinant of human character in the molecular architecture of DNA, biology may or must encounter its own revolutionary principle of uncertainty.

Twenty-five years ago, the perceptive medical biologist René Dubos punctured the widely held thesis that "scientific medicine" was responsible for wiping out or diminishing such great scourges as typhus, scarlet fever, yellow fever, and diphtheria. Rather, he pointed out, the improvement resulted largely from the great humanitarian social reforms of the nineteenth century, which rapidly evolved into public health practices that brought about spectacular improvements in the sanitary and nutritional state of the Western world. This achievement, he wrote, "cannot be credited to the type of laboratory science with which we are familiar today." Instead, it was "the expression of an attitude which is almost completely foreign to the modern laboratory scientist." And he concluded,

Exact sciences give correct answers to certain aspects of life problems, but very incomplete answers. It is important of course to count and measure what is countable and measurable, but the most precious values in human life are aspirations which laboratory experiments cannot yet reproduce. As Haeckel pointed out, Richtigkeit—correctness—is not sufficient to reach Wahrheit—the real truth.[13]

In tomorrow's world the "real truth" may be very different from the view still holding that human beings are basically physical. In penetrating to such a reality, love may be a more exact instrument than chemical analysis or genetic experimentation, as Dubos recognized.

Even the present scientific world picture holds faint indications of this fact, and more can be expected. Meanwhile, the Christian healing that draws power from deep wellsprings of spiritual perception has a vital part to play in bringing forth that larger science of which Erwin Schrödinger—one of this century's great physicists—could write: "We must be prepared to find a new type of physical law prevailing in it. Or are we to term it a non-physical, not to say a super-physical law?"[14] The Christian has the right to ask: Are we prepared to find that the ultimate science of healing is one with the ultimate art of living—a living out from the divine Spirit or infinite Love we call God?

Werner Heisenberg, the begetter of the uncertainty principle, was asked by Wolfgang Pauli, "Do you believe in a personal God?" Heisenberg replied,

May I rephrase your question? . . . I myself should prefer the following formulation: Can you, or anyone else, reach the central order of things or events, whose existence seems beyond doubt, as directly as you can reach the soul of another human being? I am using the term "soul" quite deliberately so as not to be misunderstood. If you put your question like that, I would say yes.[15]

To reach the "soul" of a fellow being. Here is the touch of divinity that makes some measure of communication possible between the scientific humanist and the spiritual healer. The "central order of things" so dear to Heisenberg is not to be equated with a hypothetical unified field theory, the ultimate mathematical simplification for which Einstein searched so long without success. But it may perhaps be glimpsed in the endearing humanity of Einstein *the man*, the generous-hearted cherisher of humane values, who after attending a Wednesday testimony meeting at a Christian Science church in New York City could remark to a member who greeted him as he left, "Do you people realize what a wonderful thing you have?"[16]

A wonderful universe may well contain many spiritual wonders unexplainable by current scientific theories. The great surprises lie beyond the piecemeal reductionist empiricism posited on a mechanistic universe. The holistic medicine of today is at least a gesture in that direction, but it falls far short of the challenge offered by Christian healing that relies *wholly* on spiritual means.

What may be our greatest need in this area of experience is a leap of thought to a level of reality beyond the reach of our present scientific instrumentation. This reality is observable and measurable only through its effects on human lives, but even then it does not lend itself to controlled experiment or laboratory analysis.

Wolfgang Pauli who was one of the most prophetic of the remarkable constellation of quantum scientists in the first half of the century made a statement that indicates just such a leap of thought.

Since the discovery of the elementary quantum, physics was obliged to renounce its proud claim to be able to understand in principle the *whole* of the world. But this predicament may contain the seed of further developments which will correct the previous one-sided orientation and will move towards a unitary world-view in which *science is only a part in the whole.*[17]

This kind of open-ended thinking stands in welcome contrast to the scientific dogmatism that arrogantly rules out, on a priori grounds, the very possibility of such a phenomenon as spiritual healing. Pauli at least leaves the door ajar.

The pluralism of American society has always been one of its greatest moral strengths. On pragmatic grounds alone, the erection of a state religion is repugnant to the citizens of a free society. A state science or a state medical system should be equally repugnant.

It would have been absurd for the legislatures, courts, or administrative agencies of the United States in the pre-Einstein and pre-quantum era to rule out any teaching of the possible interconvertibility of matter and energy, the heterodox development (unthinkable in terms of Newtonian physics) that has actually ushered in the wonders of the electronic age. Yet current legal attempts to restrict the practice of spiritual healing in life-threatening cases rest on a dogmatic biological assumption that human beings are essentially material organisms whose physical well-being is determined by a chain of biochemical and environmental cause and effect quite as rigorous and mechanistic as that of classical physics.

As always, however, the human spirit is larger than any of the specialized activities in which it engages. In the practical interface between orthodox medicine and Christian healing, there is often a remarkable degree of mutual respect and even warm appreciation expressed on both sides, as the remaining chapters of this book will illustrate. Both approaches share a concern for alleviating the sufferings of humanity, and both recognize the occupational hazards and human fallibilities in practicing any system or ministry of healing. These common interests help to break down unnecessary misunderstandings. Here is that reaching out to the "soul" of a fellow being which Heisenberg saw as related to our reaching out to "the central order of things" for which he was willing to accept the word God.[18] In a somewhat similar way, Mary Baker Eddy wrote, "The cement of a higher humanity will unite all interests in the one divinity."[19]

If—to borrow a figure of speech used by some critics within the medical profession—the medical and health care colossus astride American society rouses alarm by its dogmatic claims, economic appetite, and built-in biases, the many devoted individuals serving it are a different matter. Doctors are people, not mere cogs in a machine, and while the prestige and the financial rewards of their work are considerable, the psychological costs are often high.

This is tragically attested by the abnormally high percentage of physicians and nurses who become problem drinkers, drug addicts, or suicides. The very dedication and humanitarian concern that many of them bring to their work can sometimes exact a heavy toll of tension, frustration, ethical uncertainty, and sometimes unjust recriminations from an overexpectant public.

One of the greatest tributes that can be paid to the medical profession is the scrupulous honesty and humility with which some of its members have faced these challenges. A revealing example is an article called "Facing Our Mistakes" in the *New England Journal of Medicine*. The author, a physician from Washington, D.C., tells in detail a few of the mistakes he has made in his practice and the guilt feelings that followed. Nothing could be more moving than his own comments on this widespread problem:

> Painfully, almost unbelievably, we physicians are even less prepared to deal with our mistakes than the average lay person is. The climate of medical school and residency training, for instance, makes it nearly impossible to confront the emotional consequences of mistakes. . . .
>
> Indeed, errors are rarely admitted or discussed once a physician is in private practice. I have some indication from consultants and colleagues that I am of at least average competence as a physician. The mistakes I have discussed here represent only a fraction of those of which I am aware. I assume that my colleagues at my own clinic and elsewhere are responsible for similar numbers of major and minor errors. Yet we rarely discuss them; . . . one would almost think that mistakes are in the same category as sins: it is permissible to talk about them only when they happen to other people. . . .
>
> The drastic consequences of our mistakes, the repeated opportunities to make them, the uncertainty about our own culpability when

results are poor, and the medical and societal denial that mistakes must happen all result in an intolerable paradox for the physician. We see the horror of our own mistakes, yet we are given no permission to deal with their enormous emotional impact; instead, we are forced to continue the routine of repeatedly making decisions, any one of which could lead us back into the same pit.

Perhaps the only adequate avenue for dealing with this paradox is spiritual. . . . The only real answer for guilt is spiritual confession, restitution, and absolution. Yet within the structure of modern medicine there is simply no place for this spiritual healing.[20]

The words *spiritual healing* as used above have a much more limited meaning than is given to them in this book, but the two uses are closely related in their underlying spirit. "Physician, heal thyself" is a must for both the medical doctor and the Christian healer. And neither can afford to stand in judgment on the other.

The discoverer of Christian Science, under severe attack from the doctors of her day (themselves regarded by present-day medical historians as having been lamentably unscientific and minimally effective in their practice of medicine), occasionally permitted herself a word or two of pungent criticism of their methods. But in general she hoped for better mutual understanding in time, and she advised her followers,

Let us be faithful in pointing the way through Christ, as we understand it, but let us also be careful always to "judge righteous judgment," and never to condemn rashly. . . . If ecclesiastical sects or medical schools turn a deaf ear to the teachings of Christian Science, then part from these opponents as did Abraham when he parted from Lot, and say in thy heart: "Let there be no strife, I pray thee, between me and thee, and between my herdmen and thy herdmen; for we be brethren."[21]

A pluralist society is at once the arena, the reward, and the penalty paid for the diversity of human thinking. But within and beyond that very mixed blessing is the Christian vision of a spiritual "kingdom" or order that is the very presence and power of God, embracing, redeeming, and healing—even while transcending—the whole human enterprise.

CHAPTER 4

Faith and Works in a Pluralist Society

Show me thy faith without thy works, and I will show thee my faith
by my works.   JAMES 2:18

Jesus, we are told, performed few healings in Nazareth because
of his townspeople's lack of faith.

On one occasion he explained sadly, using Isaiah's words,
that "this people's heart is waxed gross, and their ears are dull
of hearing, and their eyes they have closed; lest at any time they
should see with their eyes, and hear with their ears, and should
understand with their heart, and should be converted, and I
should heal them" (Matt. 13:15).

He was obviously not asking for a blind, unreasoning faith,
but that people might "understand with their heart." Committed Christian healers in a number of denominations understandably object to being labeled "faith healers." Important as
faith may be, *agape* or the Christian love so preeminently demonstrated by Jesus is even more vital, as Paul made clear to the
Corinthians (1 Cor. 13).

Today, among those practicing Christian healing there ap-
pears to be also a growing conviction that God must be understood (not merely believed) as operating through spiritual laws
and not merely from divine whim. An occasional writer may
even quote the first sentence of the first chapter of *Science and
Health:* "The prayer that reforms the sinner and heals the sick is
an absolute faith that all things are possible to God,—a spiritual understanding of Him, an unselfed love."[1] According to
this prescription, however, the indispensable elements of spiritual

understanding and unselfed love do not make faith unnecessary; they make it absolute!

At times, according to the Gospels, the disciples' grasp of the spiritual commission given them by Jesus was insufficient to bring results. When they asked him plaintively why they had been unable to heal the epileptic boy whom he himself had proceeded to cure with a few confident words, his answer was blunt:

> Because of your unbelief: for verily I say unto you, If ye have faith as a grain of mustard seed, ye shall say unto this mountain, Remove hence to yonder place; and it shall remove; and nothing shall be impossible unto you. Howbeit this kind goeth not out but by prayer and fasting (Matt. 17:20).

"Prayer and fasting" implies spiritual commitment and a discipline at least equal to that required for the achievement of excellence in any exacting human undertaking. Discipleship and discipline are closely related; study and practice are required for the mastery of any important skill. Christian healing is demonstrably not for credulous dabblers.

Again Jesus implied this in the condition he attached to one of his most quoted promises: "If ye continue in my words, then are ye my disciples indeed; and ye shall know the truth, and the truth shall make you free" (John 8:31, 32). Discipleship was a continuing task, to be tested by its fruits; and truth was to be known, not merely believed.

In today's intellectual climate it would have been even more difficult for Jesus and his disciples to carry on their healing work unimpeded than it was in ancient Judea. This time, scientific as well as religious orthodoxy would be scandalized that upstart, untrained fishermen should claim miraculous cures of cases obviously requiring the services of specialists with years of medical training and equipped with the latest medical technology.

Why, it may be asked, would a present-day disciple not be at least willing to cooperate with an expert medical team working on a difficult case? Wouldn't that actually be utilizing the best of both worlds? Wouldn't it increase the likelihood of success in a life-threatening situation?

Many spiritual healers today do regard their work as a

collaborative one—supplementing, aiding, and only occasionally replacing the work of doctors. It is sometimes regarded as filling in the gaps and correcting the errors of biomedicine. This may suggest a "God of the gaps" to some critics, but it undoubtedly has brought great comfort to many patients—and to some doctors.

At the opposite extreme are the militant faith-healing sects—often fundamentalist—for whom a physician is virtually an emissary of Satan. In some cases members of these groups are even threatened with hell fire by their leaders if they should turn to a doctor for help. In most cases their faith rests on the same sort of biblical literalism that leads them to believe that the world was created by God in seven days some six thousand years ago, with Adam appearing on the sixth day. (Since Christian Scientists are sometimes accused of a similar literalism, it is useful to note that as early as 1875 Mrs. Eddy wrote in the first edition of *Science and Health*, "Mr. Darwin is right with regard to mortal man or matter, but should have made a distinction between these and the immortal, whose basis is Spirit.") Although recognizing the sincerity and the genuine Christianity in many of these people, most Christian healers understandably desire not to be confused with them or with the defiance of law that too often marks their actions and attitudes.

Christian Science represents a third position. In general, experience has shown that Christian Science treatment and medicine do not mix well, but church members are always free to decide for themselves which form of treatment they will turn to in a given situation. More on this subject remains to be said—and illustrated—further on in this book. But for the moment we will take a quick look at the rationale for this either-or position.

Christian Scientists are apt to answer the question of why they don't try to mix their own form of treatment with medicine by pointing to Jesus' sole reliance on spiritual power and his injunction against trying to serve two masters. To understand what this means to them, it is necessary to recognize the centrality of their conviction that Spirit alone is *real* in the fullest sense of the term. Matter, on the other hand, is regarded as a false, distorted, temporal, finite sense of being, from which Christianity, "scientifically" understood, progressively frees one.

This is not a simple question of "mind over matter." The

basic distinction is actually not between mind and matter (which even physics today tends to regard as a continuum rather than a sharp dualism) but between the divine Mind (God, Spirit, Principle, Love) and mortal mind (a false mode of thinking that objectifies itself *to* itself as matter). The healing of disease is incidental to the progressive spiritualizing of one's whole life and thought.

Mrs. Eddy went so far as to write, "Healing physical sickness is the smallest part of Christian Science. It is only the bugle-call to thought and action, in the higher range of infinite goodness." To which she added a theologically expressed but psychologically realistic explanation: "The emphatic purpose of Christian Science is the healing of sin; and this task, sometimes, may be harder than the cure of disease; because, while mortals love to sin, they do not love to be sick."[2]

Commenting on the desirability of relying wholly on Spirit for healing, an official Christian Science publication puts the issue this way:

As the Christian Scientist understands it, such conformity [to God's will] includes the overcoming of faith in matter and of reliance on material means of healing. For the Christian traditionalist who believes that God works through matter it may be possible to combine some measure of reliance on prayer with some measure of reliance on medical skills. Generally it has been accepted that God creates both germs to cause disease and drugs to cure it, and many Christians are not troubled by this appearance of a house divided against itself. But the more uncompromising position of Christian Science reflects the radicalism of Jesus' words: "It is the spirit that quickeneth; the flesh profiteth nothing."[3]

This is closely akin to the position of some Church Fathers of the second century, notably Tatian, who held that

if anyone is healed by matter, through trusting in it, much more will he be healed by having recourse to the power of God. . . . Why is he who trusts in the system of matter not willing to trust in God? . . . Why do you deify the objects of nature?[4]

The general tendency of our scientific age is to write off all successful Christian healings as the result of suggestion or the placebo effect, and the diseases healed as being undoubtedly psychosomatic or hysterical. Wherever a reductionist explanation of this kind is transparently insufficient to explain a particular healing, the recovery is apt to be dismissed by the scientific skeptic as an instance of spontaneous remission. This handy phrase is one of those professional terms that William James pointed out ironically explains nothing but is calculated to shut off further examination of phenomena embarrassingly out of line with currently accepted laws of nature.

A similar tendency is to dismiss any account of a healing that has not been under clinical observation from beginning to end as mere "anecdotal evidence" and therefore automatically unworthy of credibility. This omnibus phrase lumps in one pejorative category everything from the extravagant fictions of a snake-oil salesman to the sworn testimony of a citizen of known integrity supported by impressive if not conclusive evidence and the matching testimony of other responsible witnesses.

Geoffrey Hoyland in his fascinating little 1947 book on spiritual healing wrote in regard to the problem of measuring this phenomenon:

> We are confined almost exclusively to the historical method . . . since the higher spiritual forces do not lend themselves to normal scientific treatment; we cannot lay on faith, love, and holiness in a laboratory, to be used as desired, in the same way that we can provide water, electricity, and sulphuretted hydrogen. We can usually only investigate events that have already happened, with all the uncertainty that such historical methods imply.[5]

Now that quantum theory has reintroduced uncertainty as well as subjectivity back into physics, there has had to be some modification of the rules of evidence, but the demand for evidence—even if it is only a matter of statistical probabilities—still remains.

Nor can religion escape a similar demand. In the language of the New Testament, the promised kingdom of God calls for evidence of "works" (John 14:12; James 2:18). In the language of Christian Science, the reconciliation of revelation and reason calls for "demonstration." Mrs. Eddy put it strongly when she wrote, "If Christian Science lacked the proof of its goodness and utility, it would destroy itself; for it rests alone on demonstration."[6]

In 1966, the centennial year of the movement, the Christian Science Publishing Society in Boston brought together in one volume, *A Century of Christian Science Healing*, a wide variety of representative letters of testimony selected from the tens of thousands published in the denomination's periodicals over the preceding hundred years. The foreword to the book asked, "Is Christianity relevant to a scientific age?" and the concrete experiences that followed provided their own sort of answer.

These accounts of the healing of all kinds of diseases, disabilities, and life situations are not case histories in a medical or psychiatric sense. But they are chunks of life, human documents bearing witness in a multitude of ways to the healing and transforming power of Spirit—or, as the foreword puts it, "human lives radically grasped by the Christ." The medical investigator may demand more clinical details and the sociologist deplore the paucity of statistical data, but the book and the hundred years of evidence from which it draws its examples may well be the single most impressive collection of Christian healings since the Acts of the Apostles.

Here is a current of experience—a countercurrent in today's secular culture—that by its very volume and persistence raises questions about the increasing demand of the organized medical and health care professions to be recognized as the sole authority on all matters relating to healing. This particular current or countercurrent is, to be sure, only one part of a two-thousand-year-old tradition, but its uniqueness lies in its claim to be at the same time Christian and scientific.

Its founder did not hesitate to write, "Jesus of Nazareth was the most scientific man that ever trod the globe." To which she added in explanation: "He plunged beneath the material surface of things, and found the spiritual cause."[7]

Something of the meaning of this for Christian Scientists is evident in the last chapter of their centennial volume, from which the following passage comes:

The purpose of spiritual healing is never simply to produce physical ease. It is rather to put off the limited, physical concept of man which binds thought to matter, and thus bring to light Paul's "new" man. This is the man whom Christian Scientists understand to be the "real" man, created by God in His own image, spiritual and whole.

Here is the reason Christian Scientists do not turn to a doctor if they are not quickly healed through their own or a practitioner's prayers. Bodily conditions they view as effect rather than cause—the outward expression of conscious and unconscious thoughts. On this premise what needs to be healed is always a false concept of being, not a material condition. The purpose of turning to God for healing is therefore not merely to change the evidence before the physical senses but to heal the deeper alienation of human thought from God.

This is a purpose which, as Christian Scientists view it, deserves the most rigorous effort. Their very persistence in holding to what they call the truth of being in the face of alarming physical evidence to the contrary may be what is needed to bring about a healing. Testifiers sometimes express special gratitude for a long-delayed healing which has forced them to search their hearts, discipline their thoughts, and spiritualize their motives more thoroughly. . . .

In some cases a relatively minor physical ailment may require a longer struggle with ingrained traits of character than does an acute need which turns the individual more wholeheartedly to God. The newcomer to Christian Science who has experienced a remarkable healing discovers, as he progresses in his study, that the blessings are inseparable from the demands.

On the other hand, the student of Christian Science who has accepted its mental and moral discipline and demonstrated for himself the unfailing goodness of God is not likely to look elsewhere for help. It is no sacrifice to forego medical treatment when one has repeatedly proved that "the word of God is quick, and powerful, and sharper than any two-edged sword" (Hebrews 4:12). Puzzling as the Christian Scientist's confidence may be to others, it is rooted in concrete experience and reasoned conviction as well as in the Christian promises.

When due allowance has been made for the inevitable imperfections in the human practice of Christian Science and for the abuses of it by those who may claim its name without accepting its spirit or its discipline, the fact remains that it has restored the healing of primitive Christianity to a recognized place in modern society. What seemed to most people a preposterous claim when it was made by a single Christian woman one hundred years ago has been accepted since then by increasing numbers, many of them professional people trained in modern scientific method and the critical examination of evidence. Whole families have relied exclusively on Christian Science for healing through several generations. . . .

Christian Science healing is in fact one way of worshiping God. It is an integral part of a deeply felt and closely reasoned view of ultimate reality. This very fact sometimes causes its use of the words "real" and "unreal" to be misunderstood. For when Christian Scientists speak of sickness as unreal, they do not mean that humanly it is to be ignored. They mean rather that it is no part of man's true, essential being but comes from a mortal misconception of being, without validity, necessity, or legitimacy. Like a mathematical error which has no substance and no principle to support it, sickness is not to be ignored but to be conscientiously wiped out by a correct understanding of the divine Principle of being. This is the metaphysical basis of Christian Science practice.[8]

Today, however, a new dogmatism in regard to healing threatens to create a new inquisition, both of them in the name of science. A huge medical-pharmaceutical-health care industry rivaling in power the giant military-industrial complex that Dwight Eisenhower warned against years ago has increasingly worked to establish in public thought that "scientific" biomedicine is the only effective means of treatment for bodily ills—indeed the only acceptable means in life-threatening or potentially disabling situations.

The vital distinction between nonmedical treatment and no treatment at all is often completely lost by the public and the media. A newspaper story headed "Child Dies Without Medical Care" automatically suggests parental neglect and invites public outrage. Notably absent from the press, however, are any stories headed "Child Dies Under Medical Care." The tens of thousands of such cases every year are obviously too commonplace to be newsworthy—and no one is going to complain that the parents and doctors "let" the child die without trying Christian Science as a last resort!

From this simplistic faith in orthodox medicine as entitled to a monopoly on healing—and dying—a spate of legal and legislative challenges to the practice of spiritual healing has arisen in the past few years. These replicate in many ways the early attacks on Christian Science in the courts and legislatures between the late 1880s and 1910. Although medical historians today describe the practice of orthodox medicine in that period as highly unscientific and grossly ineffective, the American Medical Association of those years carried on its intensive crusade against Christian Science with the same Olympian assurance as the present medical establishment. Then as now the doctor alone was to be legally recognized as qualified to speak and act with authority on matters of health and healing.[9]

The present crusade has been occasioned in large part by the shocking incidence of child deaths in several belligerent faith-healing groups. As a result, several parents have received prison sentences of up to ten years on criminal charges because of their refusal to have medical help for sick children who subsequently died.

Even these extreme cases raise questions of constitutional guarantees of freedom of religion and statutory recognition of parental rights. But such questions become a good deal more acute when the same sort of punitive court action threatens intelligent, responsible people who have turned to a system of Christian healing that over the past century has gained increasing recognition as an effective curative agent.

According to the record, that system has won thousands of its adherents initially because they have seen it result in the healing of cases pronounced terminal or incurable by medical science. It is also worth noting as a fact of life that for many years American insurance companies have found this system acceptable in their various casualty lines in lieu of medical care.[10]

From this point on, I shall take Christian Science as my sole example of Christian healing. It provides, in a sense, the test case in our generation of a total reliance on Spirit for healing as well as for moral and spiritual regeneration. In this way it offers a more clean-cut contrast with the medical approach than do forms of spiritual healing that see themselves as supplementing but in no way supplanting that approach.

At the same time, it is important to recognize that Christian Scientists do not see themselves as taking an adversarial position toward doctors. Their one-person "Committee on Publication" in each state is kept busy explaining the wide dissimilarity between their Church's attitude and that of the faith-healing groups whose militant antagonism to both medicine and state laws has had so much publicity in recent years. There are, of course, extremes of fanaticism to be found in all groups. But the weight of evidence indicates that Christian Scientists take seriously the letter and implications of the bylaw in their *Church Manual* that reads: "A member of this Church shall not publish, nor cause to be published, an article that is uncharitable or impertinent towards religion, medicine, the courts, or the laws of our land."[11]

In short, a Christian Scientist is not "against doctors." If a member of that church turns to medicine for help in an extremity, through family pressure or for any other reason, he or she is more likely to receive compassion than condemnation from fellow members (see p. 109). But experience has shown that any attempt to combine Christian Science with medical treatment is likely to lessen the efficacy of each, since they start from exactly opposite premises. So a practitioner would normally withdraw from the case at that point, but with Christian love rather than doctrinaire censure.[12]

In their occasional dealings with doctors in matters required by law—such as reporting cases of suspected communicable disease or taking compulsory physical examinations—Christian Scientists frequently express gratitude for the courtesy and cooperative attitude shown to them on these occasions, with friendly adjustments often made on both sides. Over the years public health officials have also commented appreciatively to Christian Science church officials on the good working relations between them.

Several other points are made in a well-balanced report from the Massachusetts Department of Public Health in the *New England Journal of Medicine* of February 14, 1974:

Although Massachusetts has not always led in accommodating the beliefs of minorities, it has respected philosophic and jurisdictional limits through regulation by state and local health departments. In part, this mutual tolerance owes much to the original teaching of Mrs. Eddy. . . .

Christian Science in Massachusetts is careful to delineate the practice of healing from the practice of diagnostic and therapeutic medicine, a distinction recognized in the state's Medical Practice Act. Many conventional medical practitioners do not realize that such healing is covered under Blue Cross-Blue Shield and private-insurance-company group-health insurance, Workmen's Compensation and Social Security. . . . The Commonwealth recognizes the right of citizens to rely on God and to provide Christian Science care and treatment, even for minors, as long as the Department of Public Health is satisfied that the child is not neglected or lacking in proper physical care. . . .

Christian Scientists, in the care and education of their schoolchildren, also draw a sharp distinction, recognized by the Department and by state law, between examination of and teaching in hygiene and normal physiology on the one hand and in diseases and symptomatology on the other. The teaching of first aid is not objectionable. . . .

Christian Science practitioners advise patients of their obligations under the existing state health statutes and encourage a member of the patient's household to report notifiable diseases. In cases of tuberculosis, the patient under Christian Science treatment must be quarantined under conditions approved by the Department. . . .

These exemptions and balancing requirements are a reminder of the Department's philosophical mandate not so much to treat disease as to ensure the protection of other citizens. Indeed, remembering this philosophy, public-health personnel may be saved the temptation of trying to coerce every reluctant citizen to undertake certain health procedures and of considering less than total participation a failure.[13]

It is the virtue of pluralism that varying systems are allowed to compete on the basis of their respective merits and not on the terms set by an established monopoly armed with vast financial, legal, and media power. At the same time, Christian Scientists insist that their healing is not to be regarded as simply one more system of alternative medicine. They see it as a way of life that in its purest form shares in the spiritual depth of Jesus Christ's own words: "He that believeth on me, the works that I do shall he do also; and greater works than these shall he do; because I go unto my Father." And again, "No man cometh unto the Father, but by me" (John 14:6, 12). And because they see the spiritual healing of bodily ills as part of the total healing of humanity's alienation from the Father—the divine Principle or Soul of the universe—they see it as an integral part of their Christian life and worship.

This explains their reluctance to participate in controlled experiments involving medical observation of the progress of cases under Christian Science treatment—say, twenty cases of cancer as measured against a control group of twenty similar cases having hospital care and treatment. Suggestions of this sort, occasionally made by medical researchers, run up against a fact as decisive as the uncertainty principle for the quantum researcher.

The physicist recognizes that the very act of observing a subatomic event affects the event and thus puts limits on his knowledge. As Christian Scientists see it, healing in Jesus' way depends purely on spiritual communion with God, which is inevitably modified by the deliberate introduction of an alien purpose or method, however minimal might seem the intrusion of a medical researcher checking on the progress of a case at stated intervals. To introduce into the thought of the patient a suggestion that his or her turning to God is "experimental" would, from this standpoint, alter the character of the relationship and possibly delay or jeopardize success.

In general, one might say, Christian Scientists are more interested in proving in their lives the value of Jesus' command: "When thou prayest, enter into thy closet, and when thou hast shut thy door, pray to thy Father which is in secret; and thy Father, which seeth in secret, shall reward thee openly" (Matt. 6:6).

This attitude is reinforced by such passages as the following one from *Science and Health:*

In order to pray aright, we must enter into the closet and shut the door. We must close the lips and silence the material senses. In the quiet sanctuary of earnest longings, we must deny sin and plead God's allness. We must resolve to take up the cross, and go forth with honest hearts to work and watch for wisdom, Truth, and Love. We must "pray without ceasing." Such prayer is answered, in so far as we put our desires into practice. The Master's injunction is, that we pray in secret and let our lives attest our sincerity.[14]

This emphasis on the quality and character of lives lived in obedience to Christ is typical—whole lives, not merely occasional healings. Although the passage quoted above may look to the scientific materialist like a withdrawal into subjectivity, it has its own kind of empiricism. It demands visible results. It shares the element of pure pragmatism in Jesus' statement: "If I do not the works of my Father, believe me not. But if I do, though ye believe not me, believe the works" (John 10:37, 38).

Back in 1894, when Christian Science was under especially severe attack, William James—himself a physician as well as a psychologist and philosopher—wrote in a Boston newspaper:

I assuredly hold no brief for any of these healers, and must confess that my intellect has been unable to assimilate their theories, so far as I have heard them given. But their *facts* are patent and startling; and anything that interferes with the multiplication of such facts, and with our freest opportunity of observing and studying them, will, I believe, be a public calamity.[15]

Here speaks the voice of a genuinely pragmatic and pluralist society. And an aspiring one.

Part 2

CROSSROADS

CHAPTER 5

Test and Testimony

Early in this century when the Church of Christ, Scientist, was growing by leaps and bounds, Mary Baker Eddy wrote that "the growth of the cause of Christian Science seems too rapid to be healthful,"[1] and she requested that there be no proselytizing of members of other denominations.

When the numbers increased at an even more phenomenal rate, she took another step that illustrates the strength of her conviction that the measurement of success should be qualitative rather than quantitative. Acutely aware of the danger of pride in numbers or popularity—the mere trappings of success—she drew up a denominational bylaw prohibiting Christian Science churches from reporting for publication the number of their members.

This cool indifference to what has been called the dawning age of quantification and statistical insatiability is reflected even today in the disinclination of the Church of Christ, Scientist, to spend its energies in amassing and analyzing statistics that hard-nosed critics would in any case dismiss as based upon mere anecdotal evidence.

However, from time to time, the church has dipped into the statistical pool to answer charges made by critics. In 1954, for instance, a writer in the *American Journal of Sociology*, after examining five hundred letters of testimony in four volumes of the monthly *Christian Science Journal*, concluded that the "number of cancers, tumors, broken bones, and cases of pneumonia and acute appendicitis which were self-diagnosed by the writers seemed large." This conclusion, he frankly admitted, was based "upon impressions rather than upon objective analysis."

The opportunity for rebuttal was evidently too tempting to be passed up by the Christian Science Committee on Publication, whose manager replied in a subsequent issue of the sociological journal.[2] His staff researchers examined carefully the same four volumes or forty-eight issues of *The Christian Science Journal*. (Neither the original paper nor the staff study took account of the even more numerous letters of testimony in the 208 issues of the weekly *Christian Science Sentinel* during the same period.) The research showed that among the testimonies that specifically mentioned prior medical diagnosis there were twenty-one cases of broken bones, eight of tumor, seven of pneumonia, seven of appendicitis, and four of cancer—not to mention twenty-two of cardiac trouble, twenty-one of tuberculosis, and anywhere from one to three each of a variety of other diseases including arthritis, diphtheria, polio, scarlet fever, spinal meningitis, smallpox, uremic poisoning, and so forth.

Omitted from this count were a number of similar cases that implied there had been medical diagnosis but did not explicitly state so. Also omitted were such things as unspecified "growths" or "organic troubles" for which operations had been prescribed by physicians or had actually been undertaken unsuccessfully and in some cases repeatedly. Likewise excluded from the count were ambiguous cases such as the healing of a knee condition diagnosed by one doctor as a tubercular joint and by another as a loose cartilage. And of course the bare figures told nothing about the number of cases that were considered terminal, the number where the healing was instantaneous, the number where it was preceded by years of suffering and hopelessness under medical treatment. Above all, they said nothing of the transformation of thinking and the quality of spiritual regeneration involved in the healing.

As *A Century of Christian Science Healing* later put it, "A mere catalogue of the healings in the New Testament would do similar injustice to the spiritual purpose and power they reveal."[3]

In selecting testimonies for that centennial compilation the purpose was not to choose the most dramatic and "miraculous" ones possible. It was rather to present a cross-section of the kinds of healing going on through that hundred-year period: slow healings, quick healings; healings involving personality disorders, family problems, wartime experiences, crippling disabilities; healings of chronic ailments and terminal diseases; healings of unemployment, accident, insanity, alcoholism; healings of people full of faith and people full of doubt, of children and octogenarians, farmers and physicists; healings of situations reflecting the special problems of changing times and varying backgrounds; healings of sin, pride, indifference, resentment, fear.

In other words, the chief emphasis seems to have been on the Christian character as well as the practical effectiveness of spiritual healing as practiced by Christian Scientists. But in the two decades since the book appeared, the general situation has grown more complex. Government agencies, organized medicine, and the courts have formed a still uneasy but increasingly powerful alliance. Aided by the dubious practices of some of the more aggressive faith-healing cults, this new alliance brought about a backlash against reliance on spiritual healing in life-threatening cases.

In some cases courts have taken the position that to rely on spiritual means for healing—as in the case of Christian Science treatment—is to have "no treatment" and is thus punishable as a felony under certain conditions. The Indiana judge who announced that the "preventable death of a child will not be tolerated by the law, even when cloaked in the garment of religion" was unwittingly opening a Pandora's box of complexities, considering the thousands of supposedly preventable deaths that occur every year under medical care. And with each year the complexities grow.

The Baby Does and Baby Fays and Bubble Boys, the choice of particular patients to receive organ transplants available only to a few favored suppliants, the economics and ethics of indefinitely prolonging life in a vegetable state—these and a thousand other intricate problems make it anomalous for what has been called the technocratic imperialism of either medicine or the courts to pass simplistic judgments on the responsible practice of Christian healing.

The affidavits and other forms of testimony that follow in this book were chosen for a very different purpose from that which motivated the official centennial volume of 1966. I have selected them chiefly to illustrate some of the complexities in the interface between Christian Science (as a clearly defined form of Christian healing) and medicine in the past few decades. The emphasis is therefore on the medical aspects of the subject rather than on the religious and humane values that are particularly important to Christian Scientists themselves.

Before moving on to this collection of representative examples, I should like to quote in full a particularly useful statement of the position of the Church of Christ, Scientist, in regard to the broad subject under discussion. This statement by the editor of the church's religious periodicals—himself a fourth-generation Christian Scientist—was published as a lead editorial in the *Christian Science Sentinel* in 1984:[4]

THE SPIRITUALITY OF MANKIND

In the early years of this century, a concerted attempt was made in the United States to suppress Christian Science and render its practice illegal. Society consciously rejected the attempt on grounds that it interfered with religious rights under the Constitution of the United States.

Thinking people—including legislators, newspaper editors, state governors—recognized the threat of class legislation. They also saw that the campaign represented a form of persecution and intolerance at odds with the very spirit of a country which has its roots deep in the principle of religious liberty.

As one paper editorialized: "In this country a man has the right to worship God as he pleases. The Christian Scientist is certainly religious. His belief is a religion, and the fact that it inculcates healing without medicine, as taught by Jesus Christ, should not debar him from the protection of law, nor make him an object of tyrannical legislation."[1]

But in 1984 two mothers who are Christian Scientists have been charged in the courts of California with reliance on Christian Science instead of medical care for their children. In one instance the father of the child and a Christian Science practitioner have also been charged. Counts include involuntary manslaughter, second-degree murder, and felony child endangerment.

Parents who customarily rely on medical care have had children pass on, but neither these parents nor the medical doctors who treated the children have been charged by the state with any crime. The assumption obviously is that the proper practice of medicine cannot be faulted when it fails to heal but that a Christian Scientist who fails in some instances to fulfill the Biblical promise of Christian healing may be "guilty" of a crime.

To bring the issues into sharper focus, one needs to understand what has been happening over the past seventy or eighty years. At the time of early efforts to pass restrictive legislation, an editorial in a New Jersey newspaper commented: " . . . the fundamental principle involved is the right of the person who is sick or in pain to seek relief where he thinks he can get it. This is an affair of personal liberty."[2] It is in fact *no longer* considered a matter of personal liberty by many government officials, though this is not comprehended as yet by the general public.

Unlike the situation eighty years ago, medicine now shapes society's thought much more extensively than do considerations of religion and constitutional law. Thus medical treatment is increasingly mandated by law and government for adults as well as children. It is a trend that has foreboding parallels. In most countries where centralized authoritarian government has gained a foothold, and wherever totalitarian government has control, religious life has been shrewdly regulated and subtly diminished.

Yet at the same time there are heartening signs of currents of thought in the world that point in a very different direction. To mention only a few, there is continuing interest in Christian healing on the part of some reputable and theologically responsible Christian groups (not fringe-group faith healers). There is a growing understanding that mental factors underlie illness and health. And questions are being raised even from within the medical profession as to whether prevailing medical theory actually offers sufficient explanation of an individual's whole being to be taken as the infallible law for living that it has become.

In addition, for the first time in perhaps thirty years a new assurance that religious thought can be considered intellectually viable has begun to surface. And a hunger for spirituality, especially among young people, is rapidly increasing.

Christian Scientists are called to realize the breadth and significance of the issues that are being tested late in this twentieth century. It is not simply their own religious freedom that is in question, but the continuing development of mankind's spirituality and the survival of faith in God as something more than impractical emotion.

Christian Scientists' awakened prayer and their willingness to work are vital to the outcome. Their fidelity will determine the future of their Cause and have significant bearing on Christianity as a whole for centuries to come.

Mary Baker Eddy, who discovered and founded Christian Science, foresaw an unavoidable conflict between materialistic hypotheses and the advancing spiritual comprehension of mankind. But she also had deep trust in God's impulsion and His disposal of events. She writes in her *Message to the Mother Church for 1900:* "All that worketh good is some manifestation of God asserting and developing good. . . . conflict and persecution are the truest signs that can be given of the greatness of a cause or of an individual, provided this warfare is honest and a world-imposed struggle. Such conflict never ends till unconquerable right is begun anew, and hath gained fresh energy and final victory."[3]

Until now, hatred, prejudice, or sheer unfamiliarity has attempted to paint a largely absurd picture of Christian Science. But this need not continue as public thought more intelligently and calmly understands the issues. Mrs. Eddy once remarked at a high point of public criticism: "The combined efforts of the materialistic portion of the pulpit and press in 1885, to retard by misrepresentation the stately goings of Christian Science, are giving it new impetus and energy; calling forth the *vox populi* and directing more critical observation to its uplifting influence upon the health, morals, and spirituality of mankind."[4] And this certainly proved to be the case in the years immediately following.

The facts will come into sharper focus today also, as they did one hundred years ago. Christian Science, contrary to recent public misrepresentation, is not positive thinking, mind cure, or an alternative health care system. It is a profoundly Christian denomination, with its priority on the worship of God and the living of a Christian life.

Christian Science is not naively unaware of the human condition. It doesn't, contrary to deliberately misleading depiction, inculcate blind optimism but fosters independent thought, understanding, and reasonable caring for human needs. Since this really is the case, it must finally be found to be the fact. An individual member of the Church of Christ, Scientist, is of course left wholly free to make what must ultimately be an individual choice in regard to Christian Science healing or medicine; he or she is not under righteous judgment or pressure from peers. It is simply not that kind of church.

But those who choose to rely on Christian Science are not in their view sanguinely choosing nothing. They are choosing the tangible somethingness of divine law—the healing power of God—that has been effectively demonstrated in the lives of some families for four and five generations. In a ten-year span from 1971 to 1981, for example, well over 4,000 testimonies of healing and regeneration appeared in *The Christian Science Journal* and the *Christian Science Sentinel.*

Slightly over 1,400 of these referred to the healing of a specific physical problem. Among diseases and disorders named as having been healed were multiple sclerosis, epilepsy, curvature of the spine, cancer, cataract, glaucoma, diabetes, spinal meningitis, blindness, and more.

Out of 1,430 cases specifying a physical problem, 655 or 46 percent had been medically diagnosed, either prior to the individual's choice to rely on Christian Science or because of other circumstances beyond his control. Some 102 or 7 percent had been X-rayed, and 141 or 10 percent of the healings were later confirmed by a follow-up diagnosis. From a total of 269 children's healings, 138 or 51 percent had been medically diagnosed.

There is little likelihood that even physical evidence will convince the adamantly skeptical thought. It did not do so in Jesus' time. But because God Himself, divine Principle, is the attraction behind mankind's gravitation toward spirituality, the ultimate victory is assured. It will be hastened, however, by prayer and strong demonstration of the spiritual facts which dissolve confusion and cut through mesmeric misconceptions to reveal the naturalness of justice, truth, and spirituality.

It is a time that makes new demands on serious Christians and Christian Scientists precisely because the potential for the spiritual progress of mankind is so great. This latter part of the twentieth century requires less complacency, more continuous watching and praying, more of the spirit of the living Christ. As the Master promised on the eve of his greatest demonstration: "These things I have spoken unto you, that in me ye might have peace. In the world ye shall have tribulation; but be of good cheer; I have overcome the world."[5]

ALLISON W. PHINNEY, JR.

Here is a quiet call to arms that is more than denominational. But where are the witnesses to support its confident claims?

TWO LIVES

The first two of the examples that follow are given at greater length than the remaining ones. In each of these two cases an affidavit is accompanied by a further account giving additional details to fill in the picture. This enables the reader to see the experience more as a rounded piece of living than as a mere phenomenon of healing.

If space had permitted, I should have preferred to see this done with all the testimonies included, so that the spiritual core of each experience would stand out more vividly. But for the purpose of this book, the plain evidential value of the material seemed more important than the human interest and inspirational possibilities of using fewer but fuller accounts.

The affidavits were all furnished by the testifiers to the Christian Science Committee on Publication. I appreciate greatly the committee's permission, as well as that of the Christian Science Board of Directors and of the testifiers themselves, to use this material in the present book. It is only a fraction of the testimony on file in The Mother Church, but it serves to illustrate why intelligent people—some of them doing advanced work in the various sciences—have adopted this as their way of life.

Inevitably many of the accounts are in lay language rather than that of clinical case histories, but the actual experiences speak for themselves.

Affidavit of Doris E. Wiederkehr of Mar Vista, California

DORIS E. WIEDERKEHR, being duly sworn, deposes and says: That the experiences related in the accompanying interview are true and factual to the best of my knowledge.

My husband Elmer Wiederkehr and I were asked by an acquaintance in 1947 if we would be willing to adopt an unwanted child. We were told that prenatal tests indicated that the child would be born handicapped.

The birth took place on December 17, 1947, at St. Vincent's Hospital in Los Angeles. The delivering physician was a Dr. Buck. The child was born with multiple handicaps, including unformed vocal cords, a damaged heart, and a serious bone condition. We were also told that he had cerebral palsy. The physicians on the case informed us that there was little that could be done for the child medically and that they knew of no child born with similar difficulties who had lived beyond the age of six or eight months. We were permitted to take him home when he was five days old.

As a Christian Scientist, I could not accept this verdict. I had been healed earlier through Christian Science of a curvature of the spine and had learned to trust and turn to God. So I prayed, and my husband and I cared for the baby's physical needs as best we could.

The adoption was finalized in Los Angeles Superior Court after a six-month period. The judge at that time, after seeing the boy, suggested that he be institutionalized and offered to help us adopt a healthy child. We appreciated her concern but declined.

I traveled to the hospital with the child several times each week. These visits were required by the adoption authorities for purposes of examination and went on for several years—initially to Children's Hospital and later Orthopedic Hospital in Los Angeles. The physician in charge of the case at Orthopedic Hospital, a Dr. Pheasant, stated that the baby was too frail for surgery and that his system could not absorb medication. On the only occasion when medication was tried the boy vomited.

We received permission to discontinue these examinations when the child was between two and three. The medical prognosis at that time was that the child would never be able to speak, stand or walk properly, or receive an education. We were told that he would continue to suffer convulsions, that he had a blood deficiency which inhibited coagulation, and that the condition of his heart made survival past early childhood unlikely.

Each of these conditions was healed—through prayer, love, and hard work. He stood for the first time when he was three. He began to talk at about age four. He gradually learned to walk over the next few years, though it wasn't until his teens that he finally became fully coordinated. The blood problem was healed after a crisis when he was five. He never bled abnormally thereafter. The convulsions ceased by the time he was three.

When he was eight he suffered what appeared to be a serious heart difficulty. Because of our legal obligations as adoptive parents I called Orthopedic Hospital. Cardiograph tests were taken at our home, and I was told that the boy's chances of survival were slim. But again he responded to prayer. After being unconscious for six hours he awoke naturally. No medical treatment was given and no further heart difficulties were experienced. He went on to an active and vigorous childhood. A year later he swam and came in second in a long-distance ocean race held at Venice Beach, California, qualifying for the local Junior Lifeguard program.

Les went to several special schools for intermittent periods when he was younger and received a great deal of tutoring at home. I obtained home study materials on which we worked together. A tutor from the local Board of Education also came to the house once each week for several years to work with him. Because of his medical history, however, he was not permitted to enroll in regular public school classes. In order to obtain credits for his high school diploma, he attended adult classes and night school at Venice High School. He received the diploma in January 1975.

Les is today healthy, happily married, and fully employed in a plumbing firm. These experiences strengthened us all in the family. My husband has become a devoted church member, and I have since entered the full-time public practice of Christian Science healing.

I, Doris E. Wiederkehr . . . Mar Vista, California, 90066, U.S.A., being first sworn on my oath, hereby acknowledge that the above testimony is true and accurate in all respects.

> *Doris E. Wiederkehr*
> Affiant

Sworn and subscribed to before me this 12th day of March, 1983.

> *Helen G. Walters*
> Notary Public

My Commission Expires:
August 9, 1985

Interview with Mrs. Wiederkehr in 1983 by staff member of the Christian Science Committee on Publication

MRS. W: We had the opportunity years ago to adopt a child who the doctor knew ahead of time was damaged. But we felt that this came to our experience to bless us and bless him, and we never hesitated.

INT.: Now what do you mean by damaged?

MRS. W: When he was born, why he was—vocal cords weren't formed, a damaged heart, bones were, I forget the term they used, but not formed right, porous, the hips especially. They didn't think he would even live six months, eight at the most.

INT.: But you still thought you wanted to adopt him?

MRS. W: Yes, we were urged by the attorney and the welfare to take a healthy child. That this child would be better off put in an institution from the beginning. That it would take too much time. We had a boy at the time six-and-a-half-years old.

INT.: You were Christian Scientists at the time?

MRS. W: That's right. I was a student of Christian Science and my six-and-a-half-year-old boy was in the Sunday School. My husband was reaching out, reading Mrs. Eddy's *Miscellaneous Writings*. But he hadn't become a church member yet.

INT.: What happened when you took this baby home?

MRS. W: Well, he had a difficulty in breathing. It was hard for him to eat. He couldn't—things got caught in his throat. He couldn't walk. He was in bed most of the time the first few years. In his carriage and from his bed, he could pull himself with one arm on the floor.

INT.: When many people see the physical form, this is where their thinking stops. How did you as a Christian Scientist view this child?

MRS. W: I'll have to admit that the physical deformities didn't bother me. I really didn't see them the way some others did. He had a beautiful smile. He had beautiful blue eyes. He responded to love. And I fully expected—I never doubted that he wouldn't find his complete freedom. I was very busy, of course, because of the physical disabilities, but Job tells us, "He performeth the thing that is appointed for me." And I found that true many times. I didn't weary. I was up many times five nights in a row because he had convulsions too and ran high fevers two weeks at a time. I can honestly say there was no time when I felt burdened. Instead of looking at the material structure which was deformed and seemingly useless, I knew that in reality he had something far more to lean on. He just kept me trusting and expecting. You could see awareness in his eyes and that he was grasping these truths that we were telling him.

INT.: When did you begin to notice any kind of physical change?

MRS. W: I think the main healing came when I was finally permitted to stop going to the hospital. Because the child was under the jurisdiction of the Welfare Department when we adopted him, we were required to go to the hospital three times a week for examination. We went on the bus. It took a lot out of my day, and I'll admit that I would come home tired from these long trips. And the doctors were kind, but they shook their heads. They hadn't expected him to live past six or eight months; they didn't know of any other child that had lived past that with the throat condition and the damaged heart. They said that he was too weak to be operated on and they couldn't understand why he was progressing, why he was living, really. And I used to wonder why I had to keep going.

INT.:   But you did have to keep going because of the adoption procedures?

MRS. W: That's right. And then I finally went to the attorney. Well, no. I finally said to the hospital, he needs a rest and he can't stand these braces any longer. They didn't realize that he was fighting them so and that they were bothering him. They had tried casts at first, on both legs, but he had collapsed before I got to the door of the hospital to leave. His heart, they said, wasn't strong enough to take the weight. And then they had to use the braces and he had to have them day and night. So I phoned the hospital and said, I've just got to give him a rest. And that I would take the responsibility if they would allow the braces to be removed. So they said that I could if I'd call each day and report.

INT.:   How old was he at this time?

MRS. W: Probably two or two-and-a-half, I'd say. Then I went back to the attorney who had helped us with the adoption. I asked him if there was anything he could do to keep me from having to make these trips. The doctors were kind. The only medication that they had ever tried to give him came out like a geyser. I was eventually permitted to rely on Christian Science with the child, without the frequent hospital trips. And in less than three months he was standing upright. He fell a great deal and we did have to pad the doorways and our furniture to keep him from harming himself. But there was a lot of progress after that. And we, everyone in the family, talked with him whether he answered or not. We gave him time to answer. And I really feel that he felt that he was in on all the conversations at the table or in the car, you know, wherever we were. He always had his turn. And we could tell by the expression on his face what he was thinking. We just never treated him as though he didn't talk.

INT.: And how old was he at this time?

MRS. W: He was about four then. We took a six- or eight-week trip at one point because the children were beginning to tease him a little in the neighborhood and we thought he needed a change and needed to be away from that. We had already applied to get him into a school for children from Christian Science families. Into the four-and-a-half-year-old's nursery, because we thought he needed to be with other children, but children that would be understanding, and not force him to do what he wasn't able to do yet or make fun of what he couldn't do. The school wasn't able to take him right away. As the next step, it unfolded for us to take this trip. Everybody on vacation is in a vacation mood, so no matter who we met, they were wonderful to both of the boys. And most people like to talk, so no one realized that he didn't talk. And no one made fun of him because he was very bright looking and joined in with everything. My husband never minded carrying him. In fact he carried him five miles on one of the hikes that we went on. He was a part of the family all the time. He was never treated differently. On the way back, he improved. He gained weight and he looked more like a little boy who was nearing four-and-a-half should. And on the day we came home, the boys were tired, of course, and took a nap, and I washed the clothes and did the things necessary. Then I decided to lie down too. My husband had taken the car to a garage. So we were all asleep when a man entered our home. I believe that my younger boy must have seen the shadow of this man on the wall. And he knew it wasn't his daddy. I'm assuming this, for when I heard this shaky little voice, I saw the shadow of the man and the man in my room. Les was on the floor in the hall looking up at this man who was up tight against my dresser and just inside my door. The back of the man's head was facing me. So neither Les nor the man knew I had awakened. I heard my son, Les, saying in a shaky voice, "No other gods before you. You don't belong in here." No, these weren't the words of the first Commandment, but the power of the first Commandment was in the words. And then he repeated it again in a very firm, strong voice. And the man walked out—never touched anything—walked around the boy and walked on out of the house.

I was filled with such gratitude that I really reached out to God so that I wouldn't spoil this sense of his oneness with the Father. Because he didn't act like—he acted like he'd always talked. And I could have spoiled things by saying anything. The words that came to me were Psalms 46:10: "Be still, and know that I am God." And I was accepting it literally and spiritually. I was really being still and listening. Les went on to get a drink of water and went back to bed. All this took considerable time because he still couldn't walk that well. And when he got back into bed, he said, "Mommy, can I come lay with you?" And I said yes. And he came in and I still was listening to God because I didn't want to say anything that would make him think that it was unnatural to talk. I didn't want to make too much out of this healing that we had expected. I wanted to treat it naturally. So he got in bed and he said, "I didn't like that dirty man." And I said, "Honey, you healed that man. He won't want to ever go into anybody's house again, and I don't think he'll ever be dirty again. You made him think about God and made him know that somebody cared about him." So he just said "Oh" and went back to sleep.

Well, I lay there probably ten minutes being grateful. I would have liked to have taken him in my arms and danced around the house with him but, you know, I controlled all of that. And in a little while when I was beginning to make dinner, about twenty minutes passed, I believe, when my neighbor across the street came over and she said, "How on earth did you have such a dirty man in your house, and what did you do to him?" She said he walked up the street and never looked right or left.

INT.: What did your husband think when he came home?

MRS. W: Well when my husband came home the kids were outside, so I had an opportunity to talk to him alone. And I said, "Dad, what we've been expecting and knowing would happen has taken place. Les can talk." And he said, "Well, it's not going to make any difference. We always gave him time to talk. So we can just go on." He said, "I'm leaning on the Truth from now on." And he said, "Les is going to walk, he's going to skip, he's going to run, he's going to do all the things." From that time on he went every night with me when we walked him. We used to take him to the beach and walk him to the ocean. And we'd park the car and walk up hills with him. Let him use what he could use. We'd have to hold him on each side, but he liked to be upright like other people.

The heart condition was healed when he was eight years old. He rang the doorbell because he needed help, and when I opened the door he fell in. He was unconscious. I did call the hospital to fulfill our legal obligations as adoptive parents. They came out with a portable cardiograph, and they didn't think that he would last. I sat and prayed and read to him. When I needed to get dinner, I put on the records of *Science and Health*. He loved the chapters on Prayer and Creation. And I put that on and it was playing beside his bed while I went to get dinner. When he awakened he was not exhausted like he had been from other attacks. He was just as though nothing had happened. He never had another attack after that. And then he began to swim, and he set a record in an ocean race when he was only nine. And still, I would say, he didn't have complete use of the right arm and right leg—but he swam and came in second with sixteen-year-olds and got into the Junior Guard Program a year ahead of time. He had to be ten to be in it. They let him enroll because of the swimming that he did in that race.

INT.: When did the coordination and the walking work out?

MRS. W: Well, by the time he was five he had times when he did pretty well. For two or three hours at a time he might not fall. His teacher told me that he saw him kick a ball and was so surprised. But he was fifteen before you'd say he no longer fell without warning. Even when he played baseball. He could bat a ball that would be a home run for anybody. But he couldn't count on his legs to always take him that far, because his legs wouldn't always do what he wanted them to do. So he'd make a two-baser out of it. But he was catcher on the Little League team that whole season. He loves all sports. I worked with him, worked with balloons at first and plastic things to bat at first and encouraged him because I wanted him to do the things that boys like that do.

INT.: Was there any sense of frustration or discouragement?

MRS. W: My hardest work was not to get hurt when somebody took advantage of him. That was the hardest—harder to work out than the physical disability.

We just found so many helps. I used to put little verses in his pocket to use—Bible verses from the Bible lessons that Christian Scientists study each week from the *Christian Science Quarterly*. And I'd take statements from *Science and Health* that really meant something to him. He used to pick and choose sometimes what he wanted. He used, "Be still and know that I am God" because he wanted to fight back sometimes and he knew it wasn't the answer. So he'd try to "still" what they were saying to him and listen to what God was saying to him. I always told him that God had need of him. And that that meant He had need of his thinking. And that if he wasted time resenting or having hurt feelings over people's unkindness, why, he wouldn't hear God's voice. And he wouldn't recognize his healing and his freedom when it came. He'd be too busy feeling sorry for himself. Or angry, you know. So he learned to forgive and he learned it so well that it's helped him in later life.

INT.:   Was there ever medical verification of Les's healing?

MRS. W: Yes. We went to the medical facility at UCLA at one time when we were trying to get him into a regular class at school. The doctors there wrote to the Board of Education that he belonged with other children and that the case was remarkable. They told me they could hardly believe the improvement that had taken place because the encephalograms still indicated motor damage. But at that time he was active in sports, tennis, volleyball, basketball, swimming, bicycling. Skating didn't come until he was nineteen.

INT.:   Were there other physical conditions healed?

MRS. W: This child had another problem—that even the slightest scratch bled for quite a while. His blood didn't seem to coagulate. One morning when I was washing out the sheets and bath towels and things that I had to use in the night and he was sitting in the sun on the back porch, my neighbor came over and—she was wanting to be kind—she wanted him to come over and play. I was over-protective. If he had a bad night, or he didn't seem up to par, I didn't want him out in public where he would be labeled. But she was so insistent that I let her take him, and in less than twenty minutes he had fallen on the sprinkler head in her yard. They hadn't witnessed it. There were seven mothers over there and then some other children. They hadn't witnessed what had happened. They just saw the blood and became hysterical. This woman next door—she must have reached up to God, because she said to him, "Honey, Les, doesn't your mother tell you God is Love?" And this put him back on the beam. The bleeding stopped—just like he had turned a faucet off. It's only two or three years ago that one neighbor who'd moved quite a distance away was back and said she had never forgotten that. She witnessed it and she said any time anyone didn't believe in prayer, she was always able to tell them how steadfast this family had been that she had lived near at one time. And how she had witnessed this healing of his bleeding. He never had it again.

INT.: What do you feel you learned from these experiences?

MRS. W: In the beginning we did think human love was going to be enough. When we first knew we were going to take this little child into our home and have him, we thought we could just love him out of anything. And we had to learn that divine Love—you need the human love, but divine Love does the healing. And that takes a lot of praying, forgiving, it takes patience, it takes listening, it takes being directed and allowing yourself to let God's will and not yours unfold. Divine Love is so much better than human love. But human love can't ever be absent either. We need to do the little kind things. "Do unto others as ye would have them do unto you." "Love thy neighbor as thyself." I used to tell him when he would get angry—he never got angry at a person, but he used to at times get angry when his hands would drop things, when he'd almost get a glass to his mouth and his fingers would let loose. And I would say, You are your closest neighbor. When Jesus tells us "Love thy neighbor as thyself" you have to love yourself too, and that includes every part of you. Loving the best that you're demonstrating at this moment. If we're exasperated with a friend or with a part of our body or with a lack of talent that we think we lack, or anything, we can't hear good. We can't even acknowledge or recognize it. But to love yourself is to see yourself the way God sees you.

Testimonies by John P. Ondrak and Nancy J. Ondrak of Canoga Park, California, in The Christian Science Journal, September 1982

A line-of-duty injury that retired me from the New York City Police Department left me a cripple for over twelve years. As with all such injuries, the finest hospital, surgical, and rehabilitative treatment was provided for me. Unfortunately, after three years of medical treatment, orthopedic surgeons advised me that the fractures to my feet had left me a permanent cripple.

I had progressed from casts on both feet, to a wheelchair, then crutches, and finally to two canes and orthopedic supports in both shoes. As one doctor put it, I had much to be grateful for. Initially, I had faced possible amputation of the left foot, with the bleak prognosis that I might never walk again. But I did walk again—in a laboring, halting manner, assisted by the two canes. For this I must thank the doctors who worked so long and earnestly in an attempt to bring recovery.

Then five years later, still leaning on the two canes and with supports in my shoes, I slipped and fell on the icy streets of the city. My doctor strongly advised me to leave New York for an area with a year-round moderate climate. When he warned that another fall could put me back in a wheelchair for life, my wife and I decided it was time to go. The following summer we moved to California.

I eventually improved my walking sufficiently to obtain new work. But one of the tragic effects of the injuries I sustained was the daily pain I had learned to live with. Aspirin, tranquilizers, and other sedatives were daily ingested. Sleep was difficult, and getting out of bed in the morning was an ordeal.

One morning, as I first put weight on my feet, the pain was so intense I fell back into bed. Tears came to my eyes. Then anger and resentment welled up against this tragedy that had crippled me and put an end to my career in the Police Department. I had been an athlete all my life and prided myself on my ability to tolerate pain. But this was too much. I reached under our bed for my service revolver. As I held the gun in my hand, I heard my wife quietly say, "There is a better way." I looked at her tender, loving face and asked, "What other way?" She replied, "You have tried everything else, why don't you try Christian Science?" We talked for a few minutes; then she handed me the Christian Science textbook, *Science and Health with Key to the Scriptures* by Mary Baker Eddy.

My wife is a lifelong Christian Scientist. Shortly after we met, she told me she was a Christian Scientist, that she believed God was Love and we were all His beloved children. I told her my God was my gun, my nightstick, and my shield and suggested she keep her religious beliefs to herself. Early in our marriage I read several portions of *Science and Health*, but found what it said incompatible with my thinking and so put it down.

A few weeks after I had again tried reading *Science and Health*, as my wife had suggested, I was in such intense pain that I threw the book across the room and told my wife, in some very coarse language, what I thought about her religion. She simply picked up the textbook and said, "You are not reading it correctly. All you want is a physical healing." My answer was: "I have been in agony all these years. I'm entitled to a healing. Why must I suffer like this?" She answered, "You must forget about yourself and find out about God and your relationship to Him." I almost exploded again, but as I looked at her and felt her deep love and compassion, I knew I had to try once more. I had to find an answer to this puzzle. Is there really a God—if so, who is He? And who am I and how did I get into this awful mess?

I opened the textbook to the Preface and read Mrs. Eddy's magnificent first sentence (p. vii): "To those leaning on the sustaining infinite, to-day is big with blessings." I had read that sentence previously without realizing its significance. But not this time. Now the words came alive with meaning. For twelve years I had leaned on doctors, hospitals, physical therapy, wheelchairs, crutches, canes, supports, and pills. Now was the time to lean on something much greater than material means and human will. I was filled with an overwhelming sense of peace; I knew that what I was searching for would be revealed to me.

As I read and reread page after page of *Science and Health* I lost all sense of time. What had once been puzzling and obscure became crystal clear. The Bible, the textbook, and a dictionary were my constant companions. This study, this search, was a daily joy. My thoughts began to dwell on the sustaining infinite, as each session of study and research poured in flood tides of Truth. The understanding of God as Father-Mother, as perfect Love, and of His tender concern for all His children—including myself—began to dawn in consciousness. The truth that God is All, and that His beloved children reflect His divine perfection, became tangible fact to me.

Exactly when the healing came I never knew. The Christ so filled my days with joy and peace that time simply flew by. One morning as I was shaving in the bathroom and humming the melody of Hymn No. 139 from the *Christian Science Hymnal* ("I walk with Love along the way"), I realized that something was different. There was no pain!

I let out a cry of joy as my wife walked by and told her I was healed. As we held each other, we knelt down and humbly thanked God for this blessing. That tragic episode of invalidism was a dream. Through the earnest study of *Science and Health*, an understanding of my oneness with God had been revealed to me.

Why had my early efforts with the textbook been fruitless? Could it be, as my wife said, I was only searching for a healing? Or possibly I had read the book with a critical thought. Whatever my former motives, when I put personal self aside and did search honestly and diligently, the truth that makes all men free came alive for me, as it will for anyone who earnestly seeks Truth.

This former police officer, who had been told he might never walk again, now runs three or four miles each day. As I begin my daily run, I thank God for His love, for His power and presence, and pray that I be guided to do whatever will bring glory to His name. Through this experience I have learned that God never turns His back on us. It is we who turn away from Him. We have only to turn to Him again to feel His everlasting love. . . .

JOHN P. ONDRAK

It is with great joy and deep gratitude to our Father-Mother God that I verify my husband's testimony. His healing took place exactly as stated and has been permanent.

The day I was called to the hospital, the first thought that came to me was to immediately acknowledge the ever-presence of God and to know that not for an instant was my husband outside His all-enveloping love.

When I arrived at the hospital, the doctor handed me a form to sign giving my consent for them to do whatever was necessary in caring for my husband. Because I had been raised with Christian Science, hospital policy and procedure were virtual unknowns to me. I silently prayed to God to open my eyes to anything I needed to see. My prayer was answered, for in fine print near the bottom of the consent form were the words "Permission to amputate." I told the doctor I could not give my consent to any such operation. I was then given another form that omitted the amputation clause. This form I signed, and my husband was then taken in for surgery.

I am so very grateful to have been a witness to this wonderful healing. To see my husband again run, bicycle, dance, and walk without a limp or defect of any kind after so many years of agonizing disability, has indeed proved to me that "with God all things are possible" (Matt. 19:26).

NANCY J. ONDRAK

Affidavit of John P. Ondrak in August 1982

The experience related in my testimonial of healing published in the September 1982 issue of *The Christian Science Journal* took place as described. The line-of-duty injury referred to occurred on June 3, 1955. I was climbing a fire escape ladder in pursuit of an apartment burglar when the bolts holding the ladder in place sheared through. The ladder, with me on it, landed on a concrete yard below.

I was a Sergeant in the 44th Police Precinct at the time. I was immediately taken to Morrisania Hospital in the Bronx where I remained for the next two months. There were at least three orthopedic surgeons involved in my case, including Dr. Mario Badia and an honorary police surgeon, Dr. Miller. My left foot was fractured almost completely, with the big toe facing backward, and I was told that I had suffered comminuted fractures in both feet. After surgery the doctor put casts on both feet, and these stayed on for about three or four months.

I left the hospital in a wheelchair, with the casts still on. After these were removed, I began rehabilitative treatment at St. Claire's Hospital in Manhattan. Over the next three years I was taken to St. Claire's three times per week in a police car. There I was under the care of Dr. DeVictoria, an orthopedic surgeon, assisted by a staff of nurses and therapists. I also saw my police surgeons, Dr. De Brun and Dr. Yanaka Sauer, periodically.

In the early part of 1958 I was advised by my orthopedic surgeons that in their medical opinion I would remain a cripple for the rest of my life. Because of the disablement, I was examined by a police review board of surgeons and was retired from the department during the summer of 1958. The doctors informed me that the bones in my feet had calcified into almost solid pieces, severely and permanently limiting their flexibility and motion. Until my healing in Christian Science, I took pills almost constantly—including as many as 10–12 aspirin per day—to relieve the pain.

I might just add that my interest in Christian Science was kindled by witnessing a healing my wife experienced after a can of paint remover had spilled into her eyes and face. This seemed so miraculous that it prompted me to begin reading Christian

Science literature on my own—though without telling my wife. It was several months after this, and after the conversations with her described in the testimonial, that I finally turned wholeheartedly to Christian Science and was healed.

I, John P. Ondrak . . . Canoga Park, California 91307, U.S.A., being first sworn on my oath, hereby acknowledge that the above testimony is true and accurate in all respects.

John P. Ondrak
Affiant

Sworn and subscribed to before me this 31st day of August, 1982.

Jane C. Gummo
Notary Public

My Commission Expires:
March 15, 1985

SAMPLINGS

The primary purpose of most testifiers is to express gratitude rather than convince skeptics. They are usually more interested in describing the spiritual growth that brought healing than in going into a detailed medical history of the diseases, injuries, and disabilities healed. In certain instances, backup affidavits such as the one that follows may trace with conscientious care the writer's tortuous therapeutic pilgrimage toward eventual healing. But few people have kept the kind of precise, detailed record evidenced in the following account.

From this point on, in the interest of conserving space, the legal forms of the affidavits quoted have been simplified down to the factual substance to which they attest. In several instances I have omitted the names of physicians and the names and addresses of hospitals and clinics so that no direct or indirect identification might embarrass them. The same policy has been followed throughout the rest of this book wherever it seemed likely that identification might prove embarrassing to the physician or institution named. The signed affidavits remain on file with the Christian Science Committee on Publication in Boston.

Affidavit of Mrs. Terressa J. Simpson of Lenoir City, Tennessee, in May 1982

MRS. TERRESSA J. SIMPSON, being first duly sworn, deposes and says:

That I was raised as a Christian Scientist, but for some years after my marriage stopped practicing it. I returned to Christian Science at a point of great extremity in my life, however, and was healed of a heart condition which had been diagnosed as incurable.

The problem first appeared in the summer of 1966 when I began experiencing extreme and persistent fatigue. We were living in Media, Pennsylvania, at that time, and I went for examination to the Media Clinic on the corner of Providence Road and Baltimore Pike. The problem was diagnosed as a thyroid condition, and the physicians at the Clinic prescribed thyroid medication. But this had no effect. I visited the Clinic periodically for further examination until January 1967, when one of the physicians there recommended that I see a specialist, Dr. Woodrow B. Kessler, then of the Providence Medical Associates. . . .

My first visit to Dr. Kessler was on February 6, 1967. He confirmed that I had a thyroid condition and prescribed various drugs to help control it. I continued to see Dr. Kessler or his associate, Dr. Michael S. Robbins, for further checkups and treatments twice a month through December 1967. In spite of the treatment given, my condition continued to deteriorate.

Dr. Kessler took an EKG in December. On December 20, after comparing the results with the EKG taken a year earlier at the Media Clinic, he told me that I had a serious heart condition and that I should cease all housework immediately and avoid vigorous activity.

In January 1968 I experienced severe chest pains and was taken to the Crozer-Chester Hospital in Chester, Pennsylvania. I remained there from January 28 to February 9 and was given a battery of tests. I was told that the least exertion on my part in the future might cause a fatal heart attack. On coming home from the hospital I was confined to bed except for weekly visits to Drs. Robbins or Kessler for further examination.

After another severe attack of heart pains, I was again

hospitalized in Crozer-Chester Hospital from July 28 to August 6. While I was in the hospital, Drs. Kessler and Robbins recommended that I have a special operation, then quite new. They stated that the operation, a coronary artery transplant, had been performed only about a dozen times. They indicated that there was a 50% chance of my surviving the surgery and that even with the operation I would remain a semi-invalid. When I raised a question about going ahead with the procedure, however, I was told that there was normally no chance of survival for those in my condition without surgical intervention.

I agreed to the operation and went to Temple University Hospital in Philadelphia from August 19 to August 24, 1968, for a preliminary set of tests, among them a dye test to determine if the blood was circulating properly to the heart. The tests showed no dye at all reaching the right side of the heart except through certain capillaries extending from the left side, and the doctors informed me that my main right artery was completely blocked. On October 3, 1968, I returned to Temple Hospital for further examination and, as I then thought, for the operation itself, which was scheduled for later in the month. The physicians on my case included not only Dr. Kessler and Dr. Robbins, but also two cardiac consultants from the Temple University Health Science Department of Cardiology (3401 North Broad Street, Philadelphia), Drs. M. T. McDonough and F. M. Cortes. The surgeon who was to perform the operation put me through another dye test in order to observe the condition of my heart for himself, and the results confirmed the earlier findings.

At five o'clock on the day before the scheduled operation, a nurse performed a routine bleeding test and discovered that my blood was not clotting properly. A blood sample was taken by a second nurse who found the same results. The nurses then called in the physicians on the case. I was also seen by various other specialists on the hospital staff, and after such examination was informed that I now had a blood condition for which they could find no cause. The doctors stated that with this condition I could not possibly survive surgery, and the operation slated for the next day was cancelled. The physicians continued to administer tests over the next week or so, then sent me home, explaining that they did not understand the nature of the blood condition and that they could not consider a heart operation until or unless the problem with the blood cleared up. This put me into a deep state of depression.

I remained in bed and under Dr. Kessler's care over the next ten months. My condition was such that even the exertion involved in taking a shower sometimes caused chest pains. I was taken to Riddle Memorial Hospital in Media, Pennsylvania, on April 27, 1969, after a particularly severe attack. On that occasion I remained at the hospital for a week until May 3. I was taken again to Riddle Memorial in June. My records show that I visited Dr. Kessler for EKGs, blood tests and other checks three times in June, three times in July, and four times in August. The blood condition remained unhealed, however, and Dr. Kessler indicated there had been no change in the condition of the heart.

Shortly after my first stay in Riddle Memorial Hospital, I discovered among my books a copy of the Christian Science textbook, *Science and Health with Key to the Scriptures*, which had belonged to my mother. I had not realized that I still had this book, since at my husband's insistence many years before, I had discarded all the Christian Science literature I thought I had. But when I found this copy of *Science and Health* I began to read it every day. I also read the Bible. I felt that finding the book at that time was the answer to my prayers.

I remained under medical treatment all through the summer months. My husband . . . received a transfer to New Orleans at this time. The company required, however, that he and I sign a statement releasing [it] from responsibility if the strain of the move caused my passing. Most of my medical bills had been paid under the company's health insurance plan for employees and their families, and Dr. Kessler wrote a statement on my condition for [the company's] records.

I was flown to New Orleans in September 1969. By this time, because of the blood clotting problem, I was experiencing difficulties from bleeding inside the skin, and much of my body was covered with black and blue blotches. On September 20 I went to the New Orleans Surgical and Medical Clinic . . . where I was examined by Dr. Horace J. Baltz. I went for a second examination there on October 15. At this time he told me that the bleeding condition was very serious and that I must see a hematologist immediately. He recommended

Dr._____. . . . When I called for an appointment, however, I was told that Dr. _____ would not be able to see me for almost two weeks.

On hearing this, I decided not to continue with medical treatment at all, but to turn wholly to prayer in Christian Science for the healing. I ceased taking all medication from that point on. My husband had objected to Christian Science in the past, but I explained to him that it was my firm desire to take this step. For three days I was in great pain and unable to rise from bed. I did not have a Christian Science practitioner praying for me, but held to all that I had been learning through reading the Bible and *Science and Health* in the last few months. On the fourth day I got up, vacuumed the carpets and did housework for the first time in two years. My strength returned and the black and blue blotches all cleared up with another few days. I found I could eat, move around and exert myself without pain. I never had another chest pain from that day on.

As arranged earlier, I went to see Dr. _____ . . . on October 27, 1969. On examining me he stated that he could detect no abnormality in my heart and that there was no sign of any blood condition whatsoever. I signed a release so that he could send for my records from Temple University Hospital, and when he received them, he called me in for another examination. This took place December 3, 1969, and was quite extensive. Dr. _____ stated that in view of my previous condition, he could not believe that there was nothing wrong. He took tests but could find no trace of either the heart or blood condition. I had been told that in many instances clotting problems are caused by the medication being taken for other conditions. But in my case, after reviewing the medical records, Dr. _____ stated that he could not explain either the problem itself or its sudden remission on this basis.

I should mention that I was also healed of the thyroid condition at this time, and that this same December I called a Christian Science practitioner for help through prayer in connection with an inner ear condition, Ménière's disease, which I had had for the past 18 years. This, too, had been diagnosed by physicians. In fact, for at least ten years I had been taking the drug compazine to control the dizziness connected with the disease. Within three or four days after calling the practitioner, however, I was completely healed, and the dizziness has never returned.

After this healing I joined a Christian Science branch church and The Mother Church, The First Church of Christ, Scientist, in Boston. My husband has never again objected to Christian Science. I've been very active in church work, teaching Sunday school, serving on the executive board and on many committees in the church. I also took Christian Science nurses' training and had no difficulty whatsoever performing the strenuous tasks involved. In 1976 we bought a farm in Tennessee, and I helped my husband and our son build our house. I did hard work every day for five months during the construction. Also I did all the cooking and laundry for the family besides canning food from our garden. I am now sixty, still strong and active. I cannot give enough thanks for God's love and care, and for Christian Science.

Some twelve years later Terressa Simpson succeeded in getting copies of all the relevant medical records to document her affidavit. This was no trivial achievement, for Christian Scientists who have sought to obtain copies of hospital records—especially when these showed a sudden "unexplained" recovery—have sometimes been told that the records seem to have been lost.

In the same way friendly physicians who have seen patients healed by Christian Science in what seemed hopeless situations, and who at that time have called the healing a miracle or have told the ex-patient that only God could have brought it about, have later shown a notable—and in view of today's mental climate, an understandable—reluctance to give any written acknowledgment of what they have witnessed. As the physician quoted on page 15 of this book indicated, it would be professional suicide to make such an admission to the general public and especially to one's disapproving colleagues.

One physician, in attesting the accuracy of a striking account of healing submitted for publication in the Christian Science periodicals, went on to say, "My letter is to be accepted as verification of [the testifier's] description of the accident and healing." But then he added cautiously, "No authority expressed or implied is given for publication of my verification or name."

The same sort of concern is illustrated by the experience of Mr. and Mrs. Davey as given in the next affidavit. The physician in this instance expressed his total conviction that the healing came directly from their trust in God. But as Mrs. Davey reported when submitting her testimony to the church, he explicitly asked that his name not be introduced in any public mention of the healing.

Affidavit of Evelyn S. Davey of Los Alamos, New Mexico, in January 1980

In April 1969, when our son, Trent, was four years old, on a Saturday afternoon, I put him to bed for a nap. Instead of awakening normally as usual, I found I could not awaken him after several hours rest. I then realized there was evidence of a very high fever and a coma-like condition. I couldn't get him to take nourishment of any kind. I immediately called a registered Christian Science practitioner in Santa Fe, New Mexico, who agreed to pray for him. My husband and I also prayed very earnestly for this child. Late Sunday afternoon there was a condition of paralysis evident, and the child was still unconscious. I called an experienced Christian Science teacher. He encouraged me to call the Committee on Publication for information regarding the State Laws in New Mexico which I did. In order to comply with the provisions of the law, my husband and I decided it was best to take him to the Medical Center for diagnosis at this time. The doctor on duty was the same pediatrician that attended our son at the time of birth. The physician, Dr. _____, was visibly moved by the child's condition and asked our permission to give him a "spinal tap." We agreed and after some time he diagnosed the condition as "spinal meningitis." He tried to prepare us for the child's passing on that evening. He had been the doctor for two small boys from our neighborhood street who had passed on several years before from this same disease. He told us how much sicker Trent was than _____ or the _____ child. Our son was put in the contagious ward for children. I might add he was the only child in the whole children's ward that night, so had we needed them he would have had all the attention of everyone on duty. There was absolutely no medication given.

As my husband and I turned wholeheartedly to God in

prayer, about midnight our son awakened, asked for his teddy bear, stood up in his bed and wanted something to eat. The paralysis was gone and he was wide awake. The fever remained for several hours more. We wanted to take the child home, but the doctor asked us to let him keep him through the night. We agreed and the doctor, my husband and I stayed with him through the night. After eating some ice cream the child went into a normal sleep and awakened perfectly all right the next morning.

Dr. _____ said, at the time, that he was convinced of the validity of his original diagnosis. He said that he had never seen two people take what he had told us that night and still hold so firmly to our trust in God. The doctor asked that we let him see the child in a week and we agreed. Two grateful parents said thank-you to the doctor and took our young happy son home, rejoicing every step of the way.

A week later, I took our son, Trent, for Dr. _____ to see. Dr. _____ wanted to talk about Christian Science. He was also the County Health Officer for _____ County. He wanted to know right at first if my bringing the child in to him caused me any problems with my Church. I said, "Indeed not." I did tell him of a testimony in that week's *Christian Science Sentinel* of a healing of the same symptoms of a child being healed without a diagnosis. However, I also said our child was questioning why I had taken him to the medical center since he had always been healed without seeing a doctor. Trent had been in the Sunday School regularly since two years old and loved God very much. The doctor picked him up and set him on the table, and very firmly, but tenderly said, "Trent, Dr. _____ didn't do anything to help you. It was God who took care of you . . . Now remember that!" His parting words to us were, "Oh, for more mothers like you."

The child never has had a recurrence of this condition and remains a very athletic, healthy, normal child.

The boy's father, Richard K. Davey, on the same date signed an affidavit supporting his wife's account. A final ironic touch occurred when the Daveys called the hospital to ask for a copy of the record of Trent's case. The nurse who answered the phone looked up the record, confirmed the diagnosis of spinal meningitis, then noted incredulously that the child had left the hospital one day after entering. "Obviously," she remarked, without a moment's hesitation or a shred of firsthand knowledge of the circumstances of the case, "it could not have been spinal meningitis."

The last testimony in this section is given first of all in the form in which it appeared in the *Christian Science Sentinel* November 18, 1972. As such, it would be easy for a medical critic to dismiss it as merely an unsubstantiated anecdote. However, Mrs. Benjamin's backup affidavit, with its specific details—including the reactions of two doctors and a public health nurse to her experience—shows the sort of evidence that often lies behind a simple testimony of gratitude to God for a remembered healing.

Testimony of Garnet Storms Benjamin (now of McGehee, Arkansas, then of Lewiston, Idaho) published in the Christian Science Sentinel of November 18, 1972

In gratitude to God and Christian Science, I would like to tell of a healing. When I was in high school, I became unable to walk because of pain, and the disease was diagnosed as tuberculosis of the hip and sacroiliac bone. For about a year I was hospitalized. I did not improve, although doctors did all they could. I was finally sent home for care. I was kept in body casts, and one leg became shorter than the other due to bone deterioration.

After some time, aware that my condition was not improving, I turned to God for help. I took my Bible and began reading it, searching for an answer. The answer was at hand.

Several years before, over two thousand miles away, I had met a dear relative who was a student of Christian Science. She had given me a King James Bible, and a copy of *Science and Health with Key to the Scriptures* by Mary Baker Eddy as a gift. I had attended a Christian Science Sunday School for a short time. Now, as I read the Bible, something impelled me to ask that the *Science and Health* be brought to me. I took it, and not knowing what to do next, I began to read from the beginning. I read all that day, and before evening Truth flooded my consciousness with the realization that I was completely well. The fever, which had ebbed and flowed since I became ill, vanished, and I told my family joyously that Christian Science had healed me.

The doctor was contacted. At last he consented to have X rays taken, cautioning me that the cast must be replaced within a few days. I assured him it would not be necessary. The X rays showed the healing complete, and I went home, was able to graduate with my class, and started college that fall. The limp disappeared, and the shortened leg became normal.

Christian Science has led me to a life of freedom.

Supporting affidavit of Garnet Storms Benjamin in June 1986

I was 15 years old at the time. I was taken to Orofino Hospital in Orofino, Idaho, the county seat, where the physician on my case, Dr. _____, took extensive X-rays and diagnosed the condition as tuberculosis of the left sacroiliac. He said the bone was half eaten away. I was then sent to St. Alphonsus Hospital in Boise, Idaho, under the Idaho Crippled Children's Service. I was in the hospital in a body cast from my armpits to my ankles for months. My condition continued to deteriorate, however, and the doctors felt I should be sent home to my family. As they informed my mother, they did not expect me to live much longer. My mother, Mrs. Garnet R. Hollen, was County Nurse of Clearwater County, Idaho at the time.

A number of months after coming home, when I realized that I was not expected to survive, I took up the Bible and began to read prayerfully. Several days later something I read in the Bible prompted me to ask for *Science and Health with Key to the Scriptures*. I began to read it through page by page, reading into the night. That same night I was healed. The fever from which I'd been suffering throughout the period of my illness left. It took about a week, however, before I could persuade my mother to take me back to the hospital in Orofino to have me checked and the body cast removed. Dr. _____ agreed to take X-rays, but told me not to get my hopes up. The X-rays then showed that the bone had been restored.

I received no further medical treatment for the condition. After the cast was removed, I remained in the hospital a few days until I could walk, as I was still weak from not having walked for over a year. But I graduated with my class in high school the next spring and began college the next fall. At this time I still limped somewhat and was still receiving support from the Idaho Crippled Children's Service. Thus, I still underwent periodic examinations. These confirmed the healing of the bone. The limp, too, was eventually healed.

After I was married in 1949, I was examined by Dr. K. H. Collins of Craigmont, Idaho, who later delivered four of my children. The X-rays he took did not show any damaged bone. In fact, he was doubtful I'd ever had the bone condition until he saw the medical records and X-rays from Orofino.

A further human interest detail with a nice little O. Henry twist to it is found in a supporting statement by her mother, which appeared with her original testimony in the *Sentinel* of November 18, 1972. This good lady—a skeptical district nurse—had only reluctantly taken the girl back to the hospital for the X ray that confirmed her healing. At that point, the mother told Dr. _____ that her daughter had been "healed by reading a book." To her amazement, he reached in his desk, brought out a book and asked, "Is it like this one?" The book he handed her was *Science and Health* by Mrs. Eddy.

ENCOUNTERS

The confirmed skeptic—one might say the a priori skeptic—is bound to find fault with the testimonials of spiritual healing in this or any other book. Like Thomas, he or she grumbles, "Except I shall see in his hands the print of the nails, and put my finger into the print of the nails, and thrust my hand into his side, I will not believe." So be it. The complaint is rational, if thoroughly earthbound.

But for the participants in these recorded experiences, something *has* happened. The fact is that human lives have been changed, redirected, in some cases completely renewed by events that cannot be brushed aside glibly as fatuous illusion or mere coincidence. The relatively few experiences gathered together in this book are representative of many thousands of other similar happenings that have occurred over the past one hundred and twenty years. Some of the most notable ones that I have encountered through the years have never even been recorded in writing, though the people who have experienced them have often poured out their gratitude verbally. There are always a few, of course, who go no further than to say with the man whom Jesus healed of congenital blindness, "Whether he be a sinner or no, I know not: one thing I know, that, whereas I was blind, now I see." And some who likewise go on to say after further reflection, "If this man were not of God, he could do nothing" (John 9:25, 33).

The accounts in this section illustrate various ways in which people have been introduced to the specific system of Christian healing inaugurated in 1866.

The first of them reaches back—if not to the horse-and-buggy days, then to the Tin Lizzie days early in the century when the humanitarian general practitioner bumped and skidded over poor roads to the rescue of patients in isolated households. A surprising number of doctors in those free-and-easy times became Christian Scientists. From personal observation I would say that in the present era of high technology and specialist training fewer physicians are actually converted—although more of them are ready to admit (privately, at least) the extraordinary healing power of the Spirit.

However, some people with medical backgrounds still do turn to Christian Science for help, as illustrated in several of the following testimonies. But first back to the earlier period:

Testimonial by William C. Gans (then of Salvador, Bahia, Brazil, now of Houston, Texas) in the Christian Science Sentinel, May 11, 1974

My earliest memories of Christian Science involve the family's trip to Sunday School each week, twenty-eight miles over bad roads from our home in a rural area of Pennsylvania. In winter when roads became impassable, my parents would hold Sunday School at home.

My father was a medical doctor with a large successful urban and rural practice, yet he was the one who first introduced Christian Science to our family. His enthusiasm for the truth was boundless. He was introduced to Science by the chance finding of a copy of *Science and Health with Key to the Scriptures* by Mary Baker Eddy in an abandoned bureau drawer. He was instantaneously healed of a serious mastoid infection shortly thereafter with the aid of a Christian Science practitioner.

Two healings during my childhood stand out in my memory. One was the recovery of the use of an eye that had been penetrated by a sharp stick; the other was the healing of what had been diagnosed as a broken vertebra in my neck. Both of these healings reversed the results pronounced by the medical profession based on medical examinations and X rays required at the time. In both cases there was complete reliance on Christian Science, and the healings, with the help of a Christian Science practitioner, were complete in less than a week. In the case of the neck injury, instead of serving a five-to-ten-year sentence confined in a neck cast as predicted by the school physician, I returned in six days to a full sports program of basketball, wrestling, and skiing.

Now, as parents, it is my wife's and my privilege to teach our three lively children the wonderful freedom this healing, protective truth brings to our lives. Since 1955, my employment as a mining engineer and manager has taken me and my family to various remote parts of Latin America. In fact, for the past fourteen years we have lived on a small tropical island near the Brazilian coast. Our home has been our church; and God has been our only physician.

Our experiences have been filled with proofs of God's protective and healing power. Late one afternoon our young son rode his bicycle off an embankment and fell eight feet onto a pile of rocks. To material sense the evidence was not pretty, and included numerous deep gashes on his face and scalp. Workmen who witnessed the accident marveled that the child was still alive.

My son and I declared that in reality man is God's reflection, His image and likeness, and also that because God is ever present, man could no more fall and be injured than could God, since we cannot be outside God's presence. These truths flooded my consciousness as the child and I walked home. Especially helpful was the passage from *Science and Health* (p. 470), "God is the creator of man, and, the divine Principle of man remaining perfect, the divine idea or reflection, man, remains perfect." We cleaned the boy up and a few simple bandages were applied. The next day he went about his usual vigorous activities, and in another two or three days all traces of the cuts had vanished, leaving no scars.

Supporting affidavit by the testifier's son, Carl Gans of Goleta, California, in 1980

The medical doctor referred to in my father's published testimony in the *Christian Science Sentinel* of May 11, 1974, was my grandfather, Dr. Robert Altha Gans, who had an established medical practice in Poland Mines, Pennsylvania, when he found Christian Science. His wife, Laura Buckley Gans, was a registered medical nurse, and she too became a Christian Scientist, relying on Christian Science for healing in the raising of six children, including my father, William C. Gans.

As the son who fell off the embankment as mentioned in my father's *Sentinel* testimony, I can attest to that healing, which took place in Ilha Grande de Camamú, Bahia, Brasil, in 1960, and to the fact that Christian Science has provided our family with a wonderful sense of home, comfort, and protection through the years. I am grateful to have the privilege of raising my four children as the fourth generation in our family which has had the benefit of Christian Science.

Affidavit of Mrs. Mary Luise Moore of Little Rock, Arkansas, in March 1980

My introduction to Christian Science came when I was scheduled to have my left arm amputated because of blood poisoning. I came from a family which included a number of medical doctors—my great-uncle, grandfather, and two uncles were physicians, my father, Mr. R. D. Lucas, was a pharmacist—and I knew almost nothing of Christian Science at that time. My mother, Mrs. Nell Hamil Lucas, called a Christian Science practitioner as a last resort, however, and the condition was healed in less than a day.

I was fourteen years old then, and we were living in Little Rock, Arkansas. My arm became infected in the week before Thanksgiving, and I developed a high fever. A physician in Little Rock, Dr. Compton, diagnosed the condition as blood poisoning. One of my uncles, of Pocohontas, Arkansas, made the trip to Little Rock to examine me on the Wednesday before Thanksgiving. He informed us that the blood poisoning would endanger my life unless the arm were removed. Arrangements were then made for me to enter a hospital in Little Rock the Monday after Thanksgiving.

At this point my mother asked me if I would be willing to try Christian Science. In my alarm over the prospect of losing my arm, I said I would. My mother contacted a Christian Science practitioner in the area, Mrs. Ethel Crawford, that evening. Mrs. Crawford agreed to pray for me. The next morning, at the practitioner's request, my mother went to the Thanksgiving service at the local Christian Science church while I remained at home reading *Science and Health with Key to the Scriptures*. Before my mother returned from the service, my arm opened and drained and the fever subsided. In the course of thirty minutes

I was healed. My uncle confirmed the healing, and the scheduled operation was cancelled.

Testimony by Mrs. Joyce M. Ellis of Torrance, California, in The Christian Science Journal, November 1966

My introduction to Christian Science came when our oldest child was just five and had undergone surgery for double mastoiditis. Shortly after she returned home a complication developed, and she had to return to the hospital for a second operation.

When she was released from the hospital the concerned surgeon asked if he might take her to his home for several days so that he could keep very close watch over the child. When he felt that she could come home, it was with the strict admonition that we must carefully guard against a cold or exposure to one.

In the ensuing months the child's ears would swell and the eardrums had to be punctured so many times that we became quite fearful that her hearing would be permanently damaged. Finally she contracted a fever and was so very ill that we were in despair.

One night I asked my husband if he would agree to taking our child to a Christian Science practitioner; we had both heard of Science but really knew nothing about it, nor had we had any desire to seek information. But now in our great fear we decided we must certainly turn to it since all else had failed to heal the child.

The following morning it was pouring with rain, and the child had a temperature of 105 degrees, but we knew nothing about Science treatment and thought we must actually take her to a practitioner. We carefully laid her in the back seat of the car, and I drove to the nearest town where we knew there was a Church of Christ, Scientist.

Discovering that there was a practitioner only a block away I was at the practitioner's door in a few minutes without an appointment. All this time the child had been absolutely quiet, and as I carried her to the door she seemed almost lifeless.

I shall never forget the love and understanding of this woman. I explained our ignorance and even some hostility to what we thought Christian Science was, but that we now felt impelled to turn to it for help. I said that I had previously been a secretary to the president of the American Medical Association and a business manager in a hospital and had always had great faith in medicine until this trial, and it had been of no avail in curing our daughter.

The practitioner told me that she had been a medical nurse, her father and brother were both doctors, but that Christian Science had saved her life.

She began to explain Christian Science to me and to assure me that our little girl was right now the perfect image and likeness of God. All this time the child was lying quietly in my arms with her eyes closed, but she suddenly sat up and asked the practitioner, "Can I go to school tomorrow?"

The answer was, "Certainly, dear, if Mother agrees."

The child had been promised that she could go to kindergarten when she was five, but her birthday had long since come and gone, and she had been too ill to start. I remember being a little shocked at the practitioner's answer and actually aware that the responsibility seemed to be mine if our little one was to go to school the next day!

But from that moment the child sat up and took an active part in our questions and answers; and when we were ready to leave, she declared she could walk! It was truly an inspiring and humbling experience. She sat in the front seat and talked all the way home about what we had learned. Her father was amazed at the change in her appearance and actions.

The next morning I was startled to hear her calling me. I had had my first uninterrupted night's sleep in many months, and I ran to her room to find her up and dressing. She was all excited and she exclaimed: "That lady certainly knew her stuff. I'm going to school today."

It seemed incredible to me, but I could see she was well; so we were soon joyously on our way to her first day of school. For the rest of the year she never missed a day. That very day I emptied our medicine cabinet of all medicine, and what a lot there was!

I shall always be so grateful for that first instantaneous healing, for it proved the availability of the Christ-power. Although subsequent problems were not so quickly solved, I was never tempted to doubt, for I knew the truth of this statement on page x of the Preface to "Science and Health with Key to the Scriptures" by Mary Baker Eddy: "The divine Principle of healing is proved in the personal experience of any sincere seeker of Truth."

In her supporting affidavit in 1980 Mrs. Ellis confirmed her testimony and added that they were living in Delmar, California, in 1929 when the healing took place, that the child had undergone surgery at Mercy Hospital in San Diego, and that she herself had previously served as business manager at Home Hospital in Lafayette, Indiana.

To save the sensibilities of some readers of this book, a few of the more vivid physical details of the diseased conditions described in the following affidavit have been deleted.

Affidavit of Effie L. Russell of Montrose, California, in March 1980

When my daughter, Mittie Muriel Russell, was twelve, she became ill with a ruptured appendix. She was bedridden for over a year, and taken three times during this period to Granite Mountain Hospital outside of Little Rock, Arkansas. This was in 1936 and 1937, and we were living in Boydell, Arkansas. The first time she was taken to the hospital, she was there for four months. We were told that she needed an operation, but that her heart was too weak to survive it. She gained some strength in the first month at the hospital, then contracted mumps. This delayed the operation still further. She was finally operated on, after two months in the hospital, by Dr. S. P. Junkin of Granite Mountain and Dr. Joseph Sanderlin of Little Rock. They found, as they informed me, that she had developed peritonitis, fecal fistula, and [a badly infected] intestine. Dr. Junkin stated that he could not understand why the child was alive at all. . . . They indicated that further surgery would be needed on the intestine if the condition of the child's heart improved.

The . . . wound did not heal over the next months. The child's weight dropped from 135 to 60 pounds during this time. She lost her hair and many of her teeth. She had a high fever for much of this time. The tendons in the back of her legs became drawn, and we were told by the doctors on the case that she would never again be able to walk. In all, seven doctors were brought in on the case at various times, including, in addition to Drs. Junkin and Sanderlin, Dr. Barlow of Dermott, Arkansas, Dr. Birge of Lake Village, Arkansas, Dr. Cochran and Dr. Cone of Portland, Arkansas, and Dr. Fletcher of Montrose.

The third time I took the child to the hospital, a second . . . drain was inserted. . . . The doctors informed me that the child's bladder would be the next to deteriorate and that this could cause hemorrhaging which would lead to the child's death. In March, 1937, we took her home from the hospital. She began hemorrhaging shortly thereafter. At this point, as a last resort, my father suggested that Christian Science be tried. I knew almost nothing of Christian Science at the time, but I had, then as now, great faith in the power of prayer.

I called a Christian Science practitioner who lived some distance away. The child had been in intense pain. Within a day the pain disappeared. In three days she could sit up in a chair. Two months from the time Christian Science treatment was begun, she was taking music lessons and could sit up all day. The healing of the crippled legs took somewhat longer. She used crutches at first, but by Thanksgiving Day, 1937, she was able to walk upright.

Since this healing my family, including several grandchildren, have had many healings through reliance on Christian Science. This particular daughter, Mittie, lived a normal and active life after the healing. As a teenager she even played basketball. After her marriage she dropped Christian Science, and the many physical examinations she had in later years confirmed her healing. She passed on in 1965 from a condition unrelated to the difficulties she had experienced as a child.

In the March 17, 1986, issue of the *Christian Science Sentinel*, a second testimonial from Mrs. Russell appeared, telling of several other healings in her family. This included her own healing of what a compulsory medical examination and X ray had shown to be a cardiac asthma, several years after the experience narrated above. The doctor who made the diagnosis, she mentions, was a close friend of the family and head of a tuberculosis sanitarium in which her non-Scientist brother had recently died. The family saga through half a century suggests, like many others, that Christian Scientists have as much opportunity as any others to observe the comparative merits of spiritual and medical healing in a variety of situations.

Affidavit of Dean Alfred Sempert of Wilsonville, Oregon, in 1982

It was during World War II, while I was a patient in an Army hospital, that I was introduced to Christian Science. I was with the 328th Engineer Combat Batallion of the 103rd Infantry Division of the U.S. Army in Europe. I had been wounded in late 1944, and returned to the front in a weakened condition before recuperating fully. We were just over the Rhine at that time. The weather was bad, and in May 1945 I became seriously ill. The medics sent me to the nearest military hospital, where the condition was diagnosed as yellow jaundice with chest complications.

My condition was described by the physicians as critical. I was taken to several more hospitals in France on the way to Paris and from there flown back to the States almost immediately, bearing the tag "chest tumor" on my hospital gown. I arrived in the States at Mitchell Field, Long Island, where I spent a few days resting and was given further medical examination. After another stopover in an Army hospital in Nebraska, I arrived at Baxter General Army Hospital in Spokane, Washington, where I remained until receiving a full medical discharge with pension in November 1945.

On arriving at Baxter my condition had deteriorated sharply. I was in a high fever for several weeks caused by what the physicians described as a viral infection. In addition to confirming the prior diagnoses, the physicians diagnosed pneumonia, wet pleurisy, and tuberculosis. I was unable to get out of bed during this time, and after the fear diminished was told by the doctors that it would be necessary for me to be in bed and inactive for several years. I was also told that I would never again be able to drive a car or participate in any athletics. Since early boyhood I had been very active in this area, and I looked forward to continued participation. This information, along with the fear I felt while I had been in combat, left me very depressed.

It was at this point that a Christian Science Wartime Minister found me. A relative who strongly recommended Christian Science had been given permission to arrange the visit. The minister's first comment to me was bold and forthright in its truth: "It is not necessary for you to be in a hospital bed." This was in direct contradiction to the many statements I'd been hearing for several months. During his visits over the following months he lovingly but firmly challenged my thought about myself; and he always left me with the positive assurance that my freedom from disease could be won. He also left me copies of the Bible and *Science and Health with Key to the Scriptures* by Mary Baker Eddy. I would awaken early in the morning and read *Science and Health* under the bedsheets before the others in the ward were awake.

After the discharge from Baxter, I was sent to the Veterans

Hospital in Hot Springs, South Dakota. Still hoping that institutionalized medicine could help me, I found that my condition did not improve. I then began an earnest study of Christian Science. When not in my hands, the Bible and *Science and Health* were on the bedstand. At one point the head nurse making her rounds saw the book and asked if I was studying Christian Science. When I replied that I was, she said, "That's the way to get out of here."

Eventually, after I had begun this study, I was transferred to a Veterans hospital in Walla Walla, Washington. I remained there for two or three months, then decided to rely wholly on Christian Science for the healing. I contacted a Christian Science practitioner and requested help through prayer. When I informed the head physician at the hospital that I intended to leave and forego further medical treatment, he told me bluntly: "If you want to commit suicide, I might as well give you a gun."

I returned to my home in Portland. I continued to have treatment through prayer from a Christian Science practitioner in the area and to study the Bible and *Science and Health* on my own. In two months I was healed—and healed so completely that in January 1947 I enrolled in Lewis and Clark College and immediately started playing varsity basketball.

Shortly before I sent a letter to the Veterans Administration asking them to discontinue my disability compensation. In reply I was asked to report for a physical examination. This took place at the Veterans Administration Hospital in Portland in late 1946. The doctors had my thick medical file on hand. After a full day of examination, including X-rays and blood tests, they informed me that I was a very lucky person to have recovered at all. Of course I know that luck had nothing to do with my complete recovery. My healing came through Christian Science—from the operation of divine Principle, Love.

For the last 19 years I have been head basketball coach at the same college I attended after my healing over 30 years ago. I've experienced excellent health through the years and have continued to turn to Christian Science for healing. I'm now a member of both a branch Christian Science church and The Mother Church. . . .

There is one other part of the experience that I will mention. The wounds I had incurred during the war had left me with hand and facial scars. It wasn't until several years later—one evening when I was attending a testimony meeting at a Christian Science church—that I realized the scars could also be healed. I suddenly felt a new sense of peace about my whole war experience. And not long afterward, glancing in the mirror, I found that all trace of the scars was gone.

Affidavit of Rosemarie H. Schmidt of Trinidad, Texas, in July 1982

When I came from Germany to live in the United States, a cousin who lives here introduced me to Christian Science. She gave me a copy of *Science and Health with Key to the Scriptures* by Mary Baker Eddy with the German translation in it. Though I was not yet ready to accept all of its truths, I was deeply impressed in learning how Christian Science explains man as the spiritual child of God. Inspired by what I learned of this religion, which prominently includes the Bible in its teaching, I became interested in reading the Bible, but I did not take up the study of Christian Science at that time.

In early 1970 I developed symptoms of breast cancer. We were living in Wheeling, Illinois then. On February 17, 1970, I went to be examined by the physician who had delivered my daughter, Dr. A ____, an obstetrician and gynecologist in Skokie, Illinois. Dr. A ____, who was associated with the _____ Hospital in _____, informed me that I did have cancer and would need an operation immediately. He recommended one of the staff surgeons at _____, Dr. B ____, whom I visited at the hospital twice for extensive examination and tests in the next few days. The latter visit with Dr. B ____ was on February 21. He confirmed the diagnosis of cancer and set up an appointment for surgery at _____ for February 23, stating (as Dr. A ____ had also stated) that in his view it was unlikely I would survive for more than six months unless I had the operation immediately.

In the meantime, I had independently consulted a third physician, Dr. C ____, then at _____ Street in _____. After examination, Dr. C ____ made the same diagnosis and also advised immediate surgery.

All I knew then was to reach out to God for reassurance. It came—in the words of Isaiah 41:10: "Fear thou not; for I am with thee; be not dismayed; for I am thy God: I will strengthen thee; yea, I will help thee; yea, I will uphold thee with the right hand of my righteousness." After talking the matter over with my husband—who, though he was not then a Christian Scientist, told me he would stand by me whatever my decision—I decided to turn wholly to Christian Science for healing. On February 22, the day before the scheduled operation was to take place, I cancelled my appointment at the hospital, explaining to Dr. B ＿＿ that God would be my physician. I then called my cousin, who gave me the number of a Christian Science practitioner. I contacted this practitioner for help through prayer.

The next few weeks were a time of tremendous struggle as I sought to trust God completely and overcome fear. I began to recall some of the simple truths I had cherished when reading *Science and Health*. This helped me to put off fear and to know my true nature as the expression of God's being. Both my husband and I took up the study of Christian Science in earnest at this time. We began to attend the Christian Science church in Pallatine, Illinois. I spent many hours in prayer. After several weeks I knew I was healed, though this wasn't immediately evident from the symptoms. The physical condition did begin to change not long afterward, however, and within another three or four months all symptoms completely disappeared under the ministering truths of Christian Science.

The healing has been complete in every way. I've been in fine health since then, over twelve years now. My husband and I joined a branch church and later became members of The Mother Church. Our family of four are now students of this Science. Each day I am deeply grateful to feel the touch of God's healing Christ in our lives.

INTERFACE

Unlike the testimonies in the last section, which dealt primarily with the experiences of those new to Christian Science, the samples in this section deal with healings experienced by individuals or families where Christian Science was an established fact.

It is obvious that such healings do not take place in a social vacuum. They occur in societies where a suspected communicable disease must be reported to the health authorities, where a baby born in a hospital may be placed at the doctor's will in an incubator, where the wishes of both husband and wife must be taken into consideration when one of them is a Christian Scientist and one is not.

In a genuine Christian healing, all such factors and any other complicating elements that may present themselves are part of the situation to be healed. For the Christian Scientist that includes working out a harmonious relationship with any doctors or nurses who may be involved in the picture for one reason or another.

These brief samples provide a preliminary look at the medical-religious interface as a committed Christian Scientist may encounter it.

Affidavit of Howard L. Clarke, now of Palm Harbor, Florida, in February 1980

In Spring, 1974, my son, Terry Scott Clarke, fell out of a tree from a height of approximately 60 feet. Terry was 14 years old. The incident took place near where we then lived in Coloma, Michigan. I arrived home a few minutes after the incident to find the boy in a great deal of pain. His arm hung limp and a bone protruded (without breaking the skin) at the top of his shoulder.

Terry's mother is not a Christian Scientist and because of the obvious evidence of a fracture, we took Terry to Benton Harbor Hospital for X-rays. These showed that the ball joint in his arm was severely fractured. We were also told that the boy had suffered internal injuries, and that he would go into shock unless put under sedation. The physician in charge of the case informed us that because of the severity of the fracture and the protruding of the fragments, it would be impossible to set the bones without an operation. He stated that unless the operation was submitted to, the arm would be permanently useless.

The boy himself, however, stated that he wished to rely on Christian Science for healing. He and his two brothers, all of whom attended the Christian Science Sunday School, had had many experiences of healing over the years. He refused even shots for the pain. I had called a Christian Science practitioner before leaving for the hospital with the boy and told the doctors that he would be relying on Christian Science treatment for the healing. However, I agreed that if the boy's condition had not improved by the next day I would give my consent for the operation.

I stayed with the boy at the hospital for the entire night. Both of us prayed, and the prayerful treatment of the practitioner was continued. On the way to the operating room the next day I asked the doctor to straighten the arm and take another X-ray. He agreed to do so, and when he returned with the results told me that a "miracle" had taken place. He stated that the fragments of the broken ball joint had somehow moved into place and were perfectly set, and that there would be no need for an operation. Within 15 minutes we obtained the boy's release from the hospital. Terry wore a sling on his arm for about a week, within two weeks he was back competing on the school wrestling team.

Testimony by Lois D. Kleihauer, then of Dayton, Ohio, in the Christian Science Sentinel, May 25, 1968

All our family have had healings and have received help in many ways.

Among the healings has been one of rheumatoid arthritis. This was such a severe problem that our son could no longer walk, and a physician diagnosed it as polio and asked that he be taken to a hospital immediately. Our son had no medication at the hospital, but tests were made and the trouble was diagnosed as rheumatoid arthritis. They asked that our son stay home in bed three months and take certain medication every three hours, night and day.

We brought him home and asked a Christian Science practitioner for treatment. The boy was given no material medicine of any kind. Within a month he was back in school. The physician, concerned that we were doing our son a disservice, asked permission to examine him. We let him do this. When he finished a careful examination, he said, "No doctor, no hospital, and no medicine healed this boy. Whatever you are doing, keep it up."

Supporting affidavit of Lois D. Kleihauer in February 1980

We were living in Gates Mills, Ohio, when Brent, then sixteen, found he could not walk. We called a Christian Science practitioner immediately. Because of the nature of the symptoms, we consulted a physician to determine whether the condition was communicable and should be reported in compliance with the law. The physician, Dr. _____ of _____, Ohio, diagnosed the condition initially as polio. Brent was then taken, in March 1958, to _____ Hospital in _____, Ohio, where he was given extensive tests. The hospital physicians first told us that they thought Brent had polio, then that he might have tuberculosis of the hip. They finally determined that the condition was rheumatoid arthritis, and indicated that Brent would need to be in bed, flat on his back, for the next three months.

We were permitted to take Brent home, and continued having Christian Science treatment for him. His condition improved steadily. He received no medication, either at the hospital or at home. The complete healing took place within a month, and our son returned to school. A few days later, as the published testimony relates, the physician who made the original diagnosis, Dr. _____, requested permission to examine Brent. This examination confirmed that the condition had been completely healed.

Supporting affidavit of Brent Kleihauer of Columbus, Ohio, in February 1980

I am the son referred to in Mrs. Lois D. Kleihauer's published testimonial in the *Christian Science Sentinel* of May 25, 1968. My healing of rheumatoid arthritis through Christian Science treatment took place as she related it in the *Sentinel*.

The healing was complete in every way. I experienced no aftereffects from the condition and was very active athletically in high school that following spring.

My family had initially turned to Christian Science when I developed a severe breathing difficulty at age nine. Several doctors were consulted, but they indicated that there was no immediate prospect for a cure. My mother then called a Christian Science practitioner for treatment, and I experienced a complete healing in about a week. Since then our family has had many healings through reliance on Christian Science, and I am serving as a Christian Science practitioner today.

Testimonial by Dorothy M. Cowan of Covina, California, in the Christian Science Sentinel, *September 26, 1977*

It is with great humility that I offer this testimony. I was raised in Christian Science from a small child, and most problems have yielded quickly after dedicated study of the truths of Christian Science. Complete faith in God's power reversed quickly the medical diagnosis that one of our children was born a blue baby and had little chance for survival. The infant was brought home perfectly healed in less than a week. The attending physician admitted God's power had produced the healing.

Supporting affidavit by Dorothy M. Cowan in 1980

When our son . . . was born in October, 1955, my husband and I were told by the attending physician that the child was a blue baby and had little chance for survival. I gave birth to the child at Beverly Community Hospital in Montebello, California, and learned of the boy's condition on the morning after the birth. The physician on the case, Dr. _____, explained that the child's heart was seriously impaired and indicated that there was nothing he could do medically to help the child. He tried compassionately to prepare us for the child's possible passing, suggesting that perhaps it would be better that way for the child's sake, since if the child were to survive in this condition he would never be able to lead a normal life.

Having been a Christian Scientist since childhood, I asked one of the hospital nurses to call a Christian Science practitioner and request treatment through prayer for the child. The nurse kindly did so, and the practitioner consented to take the case. The child, who remained at the hospital in an incubator, received no medication. In less than a week, the child was perfectly healed. Dr. _____ informed us that the child was well and could be taken home. A religious man himself, he told us that the healing was surely God's doing.

This son . . . has had an active and healthy childhood and young manhood. He has participated in vigorous sports, including competitive swimming, and has never experienced any trace of the difficulties predicted at his birth.

Testimonial by Wayne N. Mortimer of Oxford, Michigan, in the
Christian Science Sentinel, February 16, 1974

Our older daughter was in an automobile accident while on a motoring trip. It resulted in a compound pelvic fracture. She was taken to a nearby hospital, where she was examined and X-rayed. The doctor in charge was considered to be a fine bone specialist. He said she would be in a cast for five or six weeks. My daughter, who was thirteen years old, decided that she would rely on Christian Science. We found a local practitioner, and a complete healing followed. There was no pain, and she was up and moving in three days. In ten days we brought her home, and she was completely active in three weeks.

Supporting affidavit of Wayne N. Mortimer in January 1980

We were living in Birmingham, Michigan, at the time, and taking an auto trip west. The accident took place August 13, 1953 [in Mendota, Illinois]. There were two cars in our party. The car in which my daughter, Elsie Mortimer, was travelling was struck broadside by a school bus. Elsie had been sitting on the side from which the bus was coming. She was taken to Mendota General Hospital. When the doctor who examined her there informed me that the X-rays showed a compound pelvic fracture, I asked Elsie whether she wished to have medical treatment or rely on Christian Science for the healing. She replied that she wished to rely wholly on Christian Science.

The fractures were set entirely through prayer, without a cast and without medical treatment. In spite of the doctor's predictions that she would be unable to move about for weeks, she was markedly improved after only three days and completely healed before school started, three weeks later. The Mendota school system later paid damages in connection with the accident, and when X-rays were taken in connection with the damage claim, the examining physician found the bones set so perfectly that he could not locate where the fracture had been until seeing the original X-rays taken at Mendota General Hospital the day of the accident.

Testimonial by Kenneth L. Shipley of Hutchinson, Kansas, in
The Christian Science Journal, September 1967

The year after I was out of high school, I was on a train which hit
a truck loaded with cans filled with gasoline. The gasoline ignited,
and the fire enveloped the train. When I heard the crash and saw the
fire, I started saying "the scientific statement of being," and the next I
knew I was in the road, and several women were putting out the fire
on my clothing. I again turned to the statement not only for myself
but for them also. I was rushed to a hospital, where I asked that my
family be notified that I was badly burned and needed a Christian
Science practitioner at once.

When my family arrived at the hospital, they were informed that I
could not live over forty-eight hours because I had been burned so
severely that if the burns did not kill me shock would. They were
advised that it would be best if I did pass on, for if I lived I would be
blind for life. The hospital reported that my eyes were burned so
deeply that they could do nothing for me; that my face was burned so
completely that I would never have a face again; and that if I did live,
it would be a year before they could graft skin or do any plastic
surgery. But they said that even with all they could do I could never
appear in public again and would be a burden to the family.

The practitioner who was giving me treatment, and who was in a
distant city, was notified of what the doctors said. Several days later
the doctor in charge informed my parents that Bright's disease had
set in and that I couldn't possibly live more than twelve hours longer.
It appeared that I had breathed fire and was burned internally so
badly that I was beyond all medical treatment. This was reported at
once to the practitioner, and the next morning there was no evidence
of the Bright's disease.

Then I had a boil, and the doctor informed me that I could expect
many more. Again the practitioner was told, and that boil was the
only one I ever had—and it disappeared quickly.

One month after I entered the hospital I was discharged, with my
eyesight restored, with new flesh where I had been burned, and with
new skin covering the flesh. No skin graft or plastic surgery was
necessary. In a few months I returned to work meeting the public, and
for many years have worked as a traveling salesman.

Sixty years after the accident Mr. Shipley, then of Roswell,
New Mexico, and his sister, Mrs. Alma I. Crosby of Gravette,
Arkansas, supplied supporting affidavits. Mr. Shipley indicated
that the incident referred to in the testimony took place while

he was traveling on a local train from Dallas, Texas, to Sherman, Texas.

Affidavit of Kenneth L. Shipley on February 14, 1980

. . . The accident took place July 29, 1920. I was then eighteen years old. I was taken immediately to the hospital in Sherman, and it was there that my family was informed that I could not live 48 hours, that I would be blind for life, that I would never have a face again, that I had developed Bright's disease, and that I would develop boils, as related in my published testimony. There were no skin grafts or other operations performed, and I was given no medication.

My parents, Mr. and Mrs. Richard C. Shipley, were then living in Kansas City, Missouri. On being notified of the accident, they asked a Christian Science practitioner to give me treatment through prayer, and came down to Sherman immediately. The family had previously lived in Sherman, and I had been on my way there for a visit when the accident occurred. The doctor on the case was an acquaintance of my parents. In spite of the medical predictions, I left that hospital after one month's time, having regained my sight and well on the road to full recovery.

Mrs. Crosby's affidavit testifies that she was sixteen years old at the time of the accident.

Affidavit of Alma J. Crosby on February 15, 1980

. . . I accompanied my parents to the hospital in Sherman, Texas, after we were notified of the accident. I was present when the doctor informed my parents that Kenneth would probably not survive the accident and of the expected dire consequences that would follow if he did.

I saw my brother in the hospital soon after the accident and was witness to his healing through Christian Science treatment. I verify the details related in his published testimony both as to his condition just after the accident and to his full recovery.

This is one of many healings our family has had through Christian Science treatment over the years. About six months before Kenneth's accident, in fact, I had been healed through Christian Science of a lung condition which, according to the doctor who diagnosed it, could be helped only through an operation and might even then leave me an invalid. This healing was confirmed in later years by chest X-rays required in my employment as a public school teacher.

Affidavit of Helen S. Mueser of Portola Valley, California, in December 1982

In about 1964 I began to have vision problems. The condition was eventually diagnosed as corneal dystrophy in both eyes. I was not a practicing Christian Scientist at the time, having earlier withdrawn my membership in the Church of Christ, Scientist, for family reasons. I had experienced some wonderful healings through prayer in Christian Science, however, so it was natural to turn back to Christian Science in a period of great need. By 1973 my sight had deteriorated to the point that I was partially blind.

I was at that time under the care of Dr. _____, an ophthalmologist associated with the _____ Medical Clinic and the _____ Medical School. He had informed me of the nature of the condition several years earlier. I was told that the disease is medically incurable and normally results in total blindness. No medication was prescribed. The one medical option which offered some hope, according to Dr. _____, was radical transplant surgery. He conscientiously explained the risk involved in such surgery, pointing out that the outcome would be highly uncertain—an all-or-nothing proposition. In desperation, however, I decided to go ahead with the suggested operations. I discussed this decision with Dr. _____. Final arrangements for the operations were to be made shortly after his return from a three-month leave.

In the interim while the doctor was away, I telephoned a Christian Science practitioner who had helped me in previous years. She was a close friend. I had begun to long more and more for the spiritual comfort I had found in Christian Science. I explained to her my dilemma and my decision to have surgery in spite of the risk. But after talking with her I found that my fear of the condition had departed. I asked her for help through prayer in Christian Science instead. Over the subsequent months I spent many hours in prayer and, with the help of tapes, in earnest study of Christian Science.

As previously arranged, I visited Dr. _____ in the first week after his return. After examining my eyes, he stated that their condition had improved unexpectedly. I did not then explain to him that I had been having help in Christian Science, but agreed at his request to return for further examination in a month. There was no further talk of surgery, nor did I have medical treatment then or afterward for the condition. I simply continued to have help in Christian Science, through prayer, and my vision continued to become clearer.

When I returned for the next examination Dr. _____ again announced that the condition of the eyes was improving. He again requested that I return the next month for another examination. It seemed wise to consent to this, since I was living in a home for retired persons in which medical care is the norm. The visits to Dr. _____ for examination went on at his request for a number of months as the improvement in the eyes continued.

I finally asked Dr. _____ why he continued to ask me to come. He replied that my eyes had been doing such unusual things that he had to find out why. I had by then told him that I was having Christian Science treatment. I said I felt that there was no need for further examinations, and he agreed. As I left the office, he said kindly, "I want you to know I am very happy for you."

This healing took place in 1973–74. I applied for readmission to The Mother Church, The First Church of Christ, Scientist, in Boston in July, 1974. I was studying Christian Science for several hours a day by that time and seeing and reading with ease. The healing has remained permanent.

Affidavit of Patricia R. Fulton of Mission Viejo, California, in February 1983

On August 26, 1967, I was taken to _____ Hospital in _____, California after being beaten in a criminal assault. The bones broken in the beating were set at the hospital and the lacerations attended to. There were several physicians on the case, including Dr. A _____. I was in a state of grief and shock at the time, but asked to be released from the hospital and cared for at home by a Christian Science nurse. In a physical examination given prior to my release, however, the doctors found what they thought was a condition of cancer of the uterus. I went ahead with my plans to go home but was urged to return for further tests as soon as possible.

I reentered [the hospital] on September 17, 1967, at the request of my husband, who was not a Christian Scientist. There I underwent three days of tests under the supervision of Dr. B ____. The results were positive. I was told that the malignancy must be operated on as soon as I had recovered sufficiently from the injuries received in the assault. Dr. B ____ said that the outcome of such an operation was uncertain but that there was no other way.

I remember saying to myself, "Oh, yes, there is another way. I am a Christian Scientist, and it is time I relied fully on God." I had been greatly uplifted by the prayerful ministrations of a Christian Science practitioner and the supporting care of a Christian Science nurse in the weeks since the assault. Thus I told the doctor that I would not be having surgery but would be turning to Christian Science for the healing. He shook his head and tried to change my decision, but I thanked him for his sincere dedication and left the hospital. My husband was reluctant at first, but I was so firm that he supported me.

We told almost no one of the condition. I remained home from my employment as an athletic director for a year-and-a-half, although I did continue my church activities. Most of my time was spent in a continued study of the Bible and Mrs. Eddy's writings, especially the chapter on "Christian Science Practice" in the textbook, *Science and Health*. I requested help through prayer from a Christian Science practitioner throughout this time.

It was in February 1969 that the complete healing came. An article in *The Christian Science Journal* was what lifted me out of the darkness into the light. All that I had been learning in the months of study came into focus. In the following two or three days I gained a new and deeper sense of God's allness and goodness and of man's completeness, never changeable. The troublesome symptoms suddenly and permanently abated, and my usual vigorous strength returned. Immediately I resumed my athletic position and even painted the whole outside of my house, being careful to give plenty of time for continued quiet study and prayer. I have been in excellent health ever since. In recent years I have even resumed participation in master's diving competitions.

CHAPTER 6

Demonstration and Accusation

A rather rueful joke sometimes crops up among Christian Scientists. Every now and then a stranger, learning that he or she is talking with a Christian Scientist, may remark pointedly, "I had an aunt who was a Christian Scientist, but she refused to have medical help—and *she died!*"

A friend of mine told me she felt sorely tempted on such an occasion to reply, "I had an aunt who was a Methodist, and she went to the hospital and had the best medical help available— but *she died*. I'm sure we can each feel sympathy for the other's loss."

I remember also a news item in a small-town newspaper headed: "Local man dies without medical care." When one read the story it turned out that the man was an eighty-six-year-old Christian Scientist. Later I learned from another source that he had become a Christian Scientist in his middle years through experiencing a remarkable healing of a terminal disease in its last stages. The result was that he had had at least thirty-five additional years of happy, productive living. But the news story noted only that a well-respected citizen had been foolish enough to die without having a doctor attend him in his brief last illness. Typically, Christian Science was presented as a villain in the picture rather than as the force that had rescued him in midlife for several further decades of Christian service to his community and his church.

To some people the death of a person under Christian Science treatment is taken automatically as disproof of its healing claims. This doctrinaire assumption reaches its reductio ad absurdum in the classic example of the medical officer who recorded two deaths from pneumonia on the same morning. In the case that had been under medical treatment, the cause of death was listed as pneumonia; in the case that had been under Christian Science treatment, the cause was listed as "Christian Science."[1]

Since no system, religious or secular, is carried on by human agents without some failures and mistakes, there is always ammunition for the attacker. But if medicine is to be judged by its successes rather than its failures, the same thing should be true of any system that over a long period of time has demonstrated its success in healing even the most desperate and difficult kinds of cases. The simple, humbling fact, however, is that no one as yet can claim a perfect record of healing—unless it be Jesus Christ himself.

The problem of failure, either in medical or in spiritual healing, becomes of particular concern when it involves a child's life. One of the toughest problems confronting traditional Christian theology has always been how to reconcile the suffering and death of untold millions of children with the existence of a loving, all-powerful God.

In the past century the advances in sanitation, obstetrics, and pediatrics have mitigated the problem in the Western world to a dramatic extent, yet in the United States many thousands of children's lives are still lost every year under medical care, sometimes despite the use of the most expensive and sophisticated medical technology. Both medical science and Christian Science are challenged to an even greater dedication to the ideal they share in common, for all their differences.

A Century of Christian Science Healing comments:

When a Christian Scientist fails to demonstrate the healing power of God in a given situation, he does not question the goodness of God. Instead he asks himself where he needs to bring his own thinking and living into closer conformity with God's law. Like the student of mathematics who may fail to solve a difficult problem through improper application of the relevant mathematical principle, the Christian Scientist does not blame the perfect Principle of being for the faulty result but seeks through the experience to grow in understanding and obedience to divine law.[2]

The letters quoted in this section are not Christian Science testimonials in the usual sense of the word. Instead, they reflect some of the ambiguities and complexities of a society whose technological convictions and religious value systems find themselves in mortal conflict from time to time.

The occasion for these spontaneous letters was a television program of the popular Phil Donahue Show in 1979 on which a young couple, formerly Christian Scientists, gave a sensational account of the illness and death of their sixteen-month-old son two years before. The little boy, suffering greatly, had had two weeks of unsuccessful Christian Science treatment from two successive practitioners, the situation worsening constantly. Finally, the parents in despair had taken the child to the hospital, where the case was diagnosed as spinal meningitis. The child was given intensive care, but a week later he died.

What made the tragic story worse was the parents' claim that both practitioners had threatened them with dire results if they should seek medical help and had blamed the parents' lack of faith for the child's deteriorating condition. The practitioners denied this accusation, and Christian Scientists who heard the program found this part of it very hard to believe, since such threats and emotional coercion would have been completely contrary to Christian Science ethics and to its general practice. The whole experience had obviously been traumatic for the parents, and their bitterness was understandable even if some of their facts were decidedly questionable. But the general impression left with the viewers was that Christian Science is a blind, heartless fanaticism dominating its adherents through fear and threats.

The following letter to Phil Donahue was sent by Mrs. Rachel Crandell, a Christian Scientist then living in Monrovia, Indiana, some time after the showing of his program featuring the young parents, Mr. and Mrs. S. While the complicating factors in the case history it recounts would not permit its publication as a testimony of Christian Science healing, the letter usefully illustrates Christian Science attitudes not generally understood by the public. The letter has been abridged.

Letter from Rachel Crandell to Phil Donahue

Dear Mr. Donahue:

I watched your show on November 23 on Channel 4 in Indianapolis with the couple whose child had died from a disease and they had since left the Christian Science church. I have often thought back about that show and feel compelled to write to you. I think of you as an objective person, seeking all sides of a point, a man who would want to be fair.

I would just like to share a very different experience our family had just this last year with our preschooler. . . .

Our four-year-old son was accidentally run over by the riding lawn mower. He fell off and the mower went over his right leg from his toes to his thigh. I was in the yard when it happened and picked him up and carried him in the house and he was crying, "I want to go to Sunday School," over and over. That little child had had proof enough in his short life already to know that his help was in God and he expressed it in that desire to be in Sunday School. His own quick turning to God was an inspiration to me. I put him in the bathtub and while singing hymns and praying with him, I washed out as much of the grass and blood from the wounds as I could. My three grade-school-age children had gone upstairs to get out their Bible and read to each other. The oldest boy called a Christian Science practitioner and his father to begin prayerful work immediately. Even though the wounds were deep and ugly, the bleeding stopped almost immediately. When his father returned home we decided to take the child to a Christian Science Sanatorium nearby to have the Christian Science nurses better clean and wrap the leg. The nursing training given to Christian Science nurses is very thorough as regards cleanliness, dressing wounds, bathing and caring for patients who are working spiritually for a healing and need help if they are incapacitated. . . .

When we arrived at the sanatorium and the leg was unwrapped, the nurses told us a very surprising thing. They suggested that we take the child to a hospital emergency room because the law in Indiana regarding child abuse and neglect is so written that if our relying on God alone to heal the leg were challenged our son could be taken from us for "neglecting medical means." We did not want to go to the hospital. We had never been to a hospital except to visit someone. . . . We came to the conclusion that if all we were seeking was cleaning and wrapping, that it did not really matter who did the cleaning and wrapping. I certainly did not fear doctors. . . . On the basis of being obedient and law-abiding, we proceeded to an emergency room. Eventually they did take the boy to clean and wrap his leg. . . .

I would like to point out here a large difference in our experience and the couple on your program. The [Christian Science] nurses and practitioner did not seek to hide the situation from us or the authorities. They did not mislead or neglect the law. They also did not make any decision for us but left the decision to us after giving us the facts. They in no way tried to make us feel guilty. I have never known of a Christian Scientist using guilt to influence another. . . .

When we asked to go home and sign the release papers, we were told that in "cleaning" the leg, they had cut off sections of flesh and in some cases down to bare bone. They had not consulted us. They just did it. Then they said grafting would be required in a few days and we could not go home. The doctor would not bring us release papers and later that evening he came to our room with another doctor, the hospital administrator and the hospital attorney and they said that if we tried to leave and take our son out of their care, they would take out a court order to keep him in the hospital until they said he could go. . . .

My husband and I talked this over and spoke again with the practitioner and listened quietly for an answer. There seemed no way for us to be free legally to take the child. We knew that if we "stole" him from the hospital, the police would come and take him back and then we would no longer be allowed to stay with him at the hospital. Since healing spiritually comes as a result of harmony and a sense of peace, we knew that chasing down the highway was not going to be a good solution. We also knew these doctors were trying to offer our son what they felt would best promote his healing. Their motives were good, but we felt they had chosen a method for us. And we wanted to choose our own. In fact we have seen healings in our family which have been unexplainable to doctors in more than one case. Christian Science has been healing people for more than a hundred years and definitely works. Seldom do we hear of all the children who were misdiagnosed, or sewn up in the wrong place, or mechanical pieces left inside them after operations. All these things I heard from other mothers while we were in the hospital. These are just unfortunate miscalculations which sometimes happen in medicine as in any other profession where mistakes are made. . . .

We decided we had no choice but to stay and continue our prayers and spiritual work and be released as soon as possible. This turned out to be 9 days altogether and during this time I discovered a lot about myself and my thinking. I also discovered a lot about hospitals. Our son was asked to undergo painful treatments which seemed very unnecessary to me and when I spoke to the doctor he was surprised as he had never even ordered such treatments and had them stopped immediately. Later he asked me to sign a consent form for the surgery of skin grafting. I did not want to do so but as he reminded me, we could never go home until it was accomplished so the longer I waited to sign, the longer we would be there. I have to say that this man was very kind and felt badly at having to force us, but nevertheless he did and he had the law to back him up. As I read the surgery consent form one line stuck out at me. It went something like this: I understand that medicine is "not an exact science" and then it goes on to say that if anything goes wrong it is not the fault of the doctor or hospital. It is incredible to believe in this country where freedom of religion is a constitutional right that the law could force me to give my son's care into the hands of an admittedly unscientific, at least uncertain, method and then promise not to blame anyone. God is the great physician. It was upon Him that we wanted to rely, and did rely.

All along they continued to check the child for many things they feared would be wrong or complicate his healing. As we continued our prayers, one by one each fear and each check proved that all was well. They felt sure his tendons were cut and he would not have the use of his toes. They constantly asked him to wiggle his toes and each doctor who got wiggled at was very surprised. They could not believe that he had lost so little blood. In fact when we first entered the hospital, they took his blood pressure and it was normal. They could not believe it and took it again, and then asked me when it had happened and were searching for explanations for how this could be so. It was so because our trust in God at the moment of the accident stopped the bleeding. They feared chipped or broken bones, so they X-rayed and found no broken bones. They feared major muscle damage but found only minor loss. Then they worried about gangrene and tested but could find no trace. In each case where they told us we would have so many days till the next step, it turned out to be sooner than they thought. The doctor spoke with us in tears and told us how sorry he was to be working against our wishes. But nonetheless, he continued his treatment. When we were finally allowed to go home he gave us a prescription which we never had filled and our son started out on the couch lying down, then he wanted to try to stand, to wear socks, boots, to try to walk, to run, to jump, to ride his tricycle, to dig with a shovel in the garden, he learned to drop kick the soccer ball. And at each new step in his healing and increased strength he would call to me or run to me and shout, "A grateful thing, Mom. A grateful thing," and then he would demonstrate how he could jump out of the swing at its full arc and land on both legs, or whatever his new victory was. "Thank you, God," he would say over and over. This true gratitude and trust hastened his healing and continued to restrengthen his trust in his Father-Mother God.

There is nothing he could do before the accident that he cannot do now. And we have all been strengthened by this experience. . . . While we were there and it had been explained to us that skin does not restore itself where there is none and that was why we needed to have him undergo the grafting, a wonderful thing happened. In the hospital's burn unit a little two-year-old had been for 6 weeks lying with burns over 87% of his body and no skin left to graft from. He had been given a 5% chance to live. The week that we were in the hospital we did a lot of praying and when we prayed for our son we knew that God's love for him was also true for everyone in the hospital and everyone in the world. That nothing is impossible to God, that if God can "restore my soul," as the Psalmist says, he can restore anything. We were told by a woman who worked in the hospital and knew of our situation that the third day we were there the little boy in the burn unit began to grow his skin back and the doctors were amazed and scratching their heads, trying to figure out some physical explanation. Of course there was no physical explanation. That was a great blessing for us to witness and for that little child.

I did not intend this letter to be so long. I just was impelled to tell you about this one experience and to let you know there are Christian Scientists who are very grateful for this wonderful teaching that helps us to prove Christianity the way Jesus did, that helps us to follow him more faithfully including his healing ministry. . . . Thank you, Mr. Donahue. If you never air anything to this effect, it is certainly up to you, but at least you will have a better perspective and hopefully be more alert in the future about checking thoroughly into a situation before airing an attack. . . .

Mrs. Rachel Crandell

One of the claims made by Mr. and Mrs. S on the Donahue Show—and on subsequent radio and television programs on which they have carried forward their crusade against Christian Science—was that peer pressure from fellow church members makes it almost unthinkable for a Christian Scientist to turn to medicine in an emergency. It is true that church members normally choose to rely solely on prayer, even in emergency situations, but this is a matter for individual decision and certainly not for punitive branch church action.

The following account, again unsolicited, was sent to the Christian Science Committee on Publication office by Jean and William E. Hawkins of Grosse Pointe Woods, Michigan. The Hawkinses belong to the same branch Church of Christ, Scientist, in Michigan formerly attended by Mr. and Mrs. S. Their experience is broadly representative in its depiction of the attitudes encountered in their own church by Christian Science parents who, under trying circumstances, have temporarily turned to medical treatment. The account presented is abridged.

Letter of Jean and William E. Hawkins of February 16, 1980 to a Christian Science Committee on Publication

In 1956 our baby girl was born very harmoniously except for a small red spot on the side of her face by her eye. As the weeks went by the spot grew larger. My husband and I both prayed for the healing of this situation. We are both lifelong Christian Scientists and had just had class instruction together while we were expecting our baby. We called on the help of several Christian Science practitioners at different times.

As a young mother I was so mesmerized by this growth that I found it impossible to see beyond this ugly thing that had grown to the size of a walnut in several months. Since this was the case, we felt it wisdom to call on the talents of a leading plastic surgeon in Detroit to have it removed. This was a difficult decision, as we had never had to resort to this kind of treatment.

Mrs. Eddy states in *Science and Health* on page 444, "If Christian Scientists ever fail to receive aid from other Scientists—their brethren upon whom they may call—God will still guide them into the right use of temporary and eternal means." Also in *Miscellaneous Writings* on page 288, "Wisdom in human action begins with what is nearest right under the circumstances and thence achieves the absolute."

This step seemed to us after much prayer and listening to be "what was nearest right."

The baby was examined and admitted to a hospital on Memorial Day weekend. The doctor chose to [perform the operation] in spite of vacation plans.

Never once during this time did anyone from 6th Church or other Christian Scientists ever make us feel guilty or that we were turning our backs on Christian Science. We never once felt that Christian Science had failed us—but that we had some lessons to learn to grow in our understanding of this great Truth that does heal effectively. It was with great humility and willingness to learn that we took this step.

We prayed in that hospital waiting room and knew wherever that child was, under whatever circumstances, God was surrounding her. Three hours later the doctor came out of the operating room with sweat and tears pouring down his face. It was only then he told us of the danger he feared. He said that she was his "miracle baby" and that the last baby he performed a similar operation on had died because the growth had gone into the brain. He had a brain surgeon standing by but didn't need to engage him as it had not developed there. We were grateful for his God-given skills in the mechanics of the intricate task he had accomplished. He expressed amazement and gratitude and we joined him in being grateful to God. . . .

After this took place we had much growing to do to reestablish our trust and faith and it seemed we needed to take one step backwards, then two forward—but forward we did go and since then have had many healings and proofs of God's healing power in raising both our children to adulthood by relying entirely on Christian Science.

In the above letter, the writers quote from Mrs. Eddy's statement in *Science and Health*:

If Christian Scientists ever fail to receive aid from other Scientists,—their brethren upon whom they may call,—God will still guide them into the right use of temporary and eternal means. Step by step will those who trust Him find that "God is our refuge and strength, a very present help in trouble."

There is no definitive official interpretation of what this may or may not mean in practical terms. This is left for individual interpretation at whatever level of spiritual demonstration the Christian Scientist may have reached, but the individual is encouraged to consider it in the light of *all* that Mrs. Eddy has written on the subject. This includes such statements as, "Only through radical reliance on Truth can scientific healing power be realized," and "If patients fail to experience the healing power of Christian Science, and think they can be benefited by certain ordinary physical methods of medical treatment, then the Mind-physician should give up such cases, and leave invalids free to resort to whatever other systems they fancy will afford relief."[3]

Also there is one clear exception to the fact that no official action is taken in regard to a Christian Scientist's resorting to medical help for whatever reason—and even then the action is protective rather than punitive. A Christian Scientist listed in the denomination's monthly directory as a practitioner or teacher of Christian Science is in a special position of responsibility to the public. If he or she is undertaking to demonstrate and teach the unlimited power of Spirit to heal the ills of the flesh, this makes a special demand for consistency in personal life and ethical standards. Thus a practitioner or teacher who feels it necessary to resort to medical treatment may be asked to remove his or her name from *The Christian Science Journal* directory for a year or two until further spiritual progress has brought or restored the full assurance necessary for spiritual healing.

The ordinary church member, including the Christian Science parent, faces a different though related challenge. Among the numerous letters and testimonials received from Christian Scientists after the Donahue broadcast, many recounted healings of their children in life-threatening situations; others spoke with refreshing frankness of difficulties encountered and lessons learned in various complex circumstances. Among the latter was one from a Michigan mother of six, written after the two parents on the Donahue program had taken the further step of bringing suit in a Michigan court against two practitioners and The Mother Church in connection with the death of their son two and a half years earlier. This woman, who divided her time between an educational career and raising a family, wrote that her letter "may throw light on an entirely different side of the question" of parental ethics and responsibility.

After listing various healings the family had experienced, she went on to tell of a chastening episode several years earlier. While doing some especially demanding academic work, she found herself pregnant once again. Her family duties plus her academic project kept her exceedingly busy, and she gave little thought to the forthcoming event. As she put it in her letter, "Since I had always engaged physicians to help with the births, I just did the medical thing, it was so easy, taking it all for granted. I did not really study [Christian Science] much and did not engage the help of a practitioner. I made the routine visits to the physician and went on with my life."

The baby came more than six weeks early. There were various complications: the physician recommended a Cesarean section, though warning of the danger because of the child's extreme immaturity; the mother, longing in her confusion to go home, be alone, and pray, left the decision to the doctor; the Cesarean was performed, and a tiny baby girl was born, only to die six hours later of hyaline membrane disease (immature lungs), "even though," as the mother wrote, "a dedicated pediatrician and personal friend of the family stayed by her side." Further excerpts from her confidential letter to a church officer follow and are used with her permission.

I am sure we went through as hellish a period as the other couple afterwards. Even though these doctors were our neighbors and friends and we knew they had used the best of their knowledge (they are *super* doctors and people) we were tormented by the fact that there had been another choice. What *if?* And especially what if we had had Christian Science treatment (we had called a practitioner at the last minute; too late). We were tremendously guilty about our own duty to our child, about the fact that we had listened to conflicting advice, that we were party to our own child's death.

Where could we turn, of course, but to God's arms for comfort and healing? Naturally we did that and, as the weeks passed that summer, the blaming, the bitterness, the guilt, the confusion passed. But I *know* what that couple has felt in the way of bitterness and blame. I felt it too. But it is *not* over Christian Science that the blame or guilt arises; the loss of a baby naturally causes these feelings.

In addition, I can say *unequivocally*, that I have never felt anything but support, help and understanding among Christian Scientists who knew our situation. They wrote, they came, they called with nothing but sympathy and support. . . . *Nobody* condemned, *nobody* felt we had failed. It would have troubled and surprised the Christian Scientists around here, anyway, to think that anyone could have anything but sympathy for a person who had passed through troubled waters. I went right on teaching Sunday School soon after that, have served as Lecture Committee Chairman.

By the way, I would have felt free at any other time to turn to medical methods if I wished. What I have valued the most about the way I have chosen is that it emphasizes the individual right of each person to grow towards God.

I am happy to tell these things and happy for the sense of confidence that Christian Science is above all *Christian.*

One more letter on this subject may be useful. Another Christian Scientist in Michigan wrote of her own experience as a mother in a letter to Mrs. S shortly after the latter's appearance on the Donahue program. A segment of this letter is given, not as being representative of medical practice, but as illustrating legitimate concerns shared by many parents of all denominations, irrespective of the method of treatment they choose.

When, on her own initiative, the writer of this very personal letter forwarded a copy of it to the Committee on Publication, she explained that her son had been born prematurely and without any apparent difficulty, but because he was only a few ounces over three pounds she had been required to release him to the neonatal unit of the hospital. The gruesome details of his medical treatment included in her letter to Mrs. S have been deleted from the following abridgment (used by permission) as serving no useful purpose in the present context.

. . . I too had a small child who passed away very early in life. In the early stage of his difficulty I was forced by state law to place him in the hands of medical practitioners in a prominent hospital, contrary to my desires as a Christian Scientist. My husband and I sat by him around the clock during this heartbreaking experience which lasted about 14 days. . . .

As the doctors were expecting, our precious one died. It wasn't five minutes after his death that the doctors were asking if we would agree to an autopsy to see what caused the death. I tell you this because of your comments re Christian Science practitioners not knowing what was wrong with your child. In our case the doctors admitted even after the death of our child that they still didn't know what the exact problem was they should have been treating. . . .

Being a mother, you might imagine how I longed to hold my child in my arms and comfort him in his time of need. I was prevented from doing so because of hospital rules. It is almost beyond my sense of human justice to think of anyone even attempting to revoke the rights of these tiny, innocent ones to have Christian Science treatment. . . .

It is not the design of this section to cast aspersions on the good faith and humanitarian concern of any of the participants in the variegated human situations glimpsed through these examples. The purpose is, rather, to challenge the blind over-simplification of a growing pseudoscientific orthodoxy that would rule out the possibility of a spiritual power transcending the limited skills of an ingenious but highly fallible human race. Since the intensive campaign against Christian Science waged by Mr. and Mrs. S arose in the first place from their young son's death from spinal meningitis, I have included several typical examples of healings of this disease in order to balance the record. See pages 74–75, 134–35, 141–42, and 175–77.

In the last analysis, the issue is Christianity itself. The letter quoted on page 112 of this book concludes with a statement of the writer's happy confidence "that Christian Science is above all *Christian*." Unless it is, it can be no more than a passing phenomenon. If it is, there is hope—and indeed evidence—that life is something more than a complex mechanism to be manipulated by clever technicians.

A final example of this Christianity is found in a testimonial published one year before the nationwide attack on Christian Science inaugurated by the Donahue show.

Testimonial of Marjorie Macartney of Palm Desert, California, in The Christian Science Journal, December 1978

Before I was born I was given up for adoption. After birth I was considered too sick to leave the hospital and was kept there for three months. Finally a nurse traveled with me to my prospective parents' home. A doctor, who examined me as required by law, had cautioned against the adoption. He said, "All her normal functions are impaired; some have virtually stopped. This child won't last." "All the more reason for me to take her," replied my mother, a new student of Christian Science. "I can give her Christian Science, and she will be healed through prayer."

She kindly dismissed the doctor, and it was decided that the nurse and I should spend the night there and a decision would be made in the morning. My mother kept me next to her bed all night. She has told me that neither of us slept. She used those hours as an opportunity to apply the truths of Science. She told me softly that my Father-Mother God was my Parent; that I was His spiritual likeness; that God was my life, my health, my all—while I looked up at her, showing signs of feeling the love and truth she was expressing. Early the next morning she called a Christian Science practitioner for treatment. That morning I retained my food; in fact, I ate everything offered me. "This baby was sent here by God for the Christian Science we can give her," said my mother. So I stayed and flourished.

Under Christian Science treatment, all my normal functions became active and normal. Before long I was plump and radiated much joy. Treatment was no longer needed. At age two and a half I was enrolled in the Christian Science Sunday School. Throughout the years I have been a devoted student of the Bible and the writings of our Leader, Mrs. Eddy. I can never express enough gratitude to God for this background. My primary healing was so complete and permanent that I have continued to have good health in every respect.

For the sake of the skeptic, Mrs. Macartney later furnished an affidavit giving the names of her adoptive parents as William Kerry Philp and Maude Louise Blakesley Philp and including the following information.

Affidavit of Marjorie Macartney in February 1980

. . . I was born in Ann Arbor, Michigan. The Philps were then residents of Grand Rapids, Michigan, where my father, William Philp, was a well-known businessman and the owner of several automobile dealerships. His brother, Arthur Irving Philp, had been a cofounder of the Dodge Motor Company with the Dodge brothers.

The circumstances surrounding my adoption and the doctor's predictions regarding my physical condition were well known in the community at the time. Many of my parents' friends were witness to my rapid healing. In later years, after my family had moved to California, many of these Michigan friends spoke of this healing when they came to visit.

My father, an Episcopalian, began attending Christian Science services as a result of this healing and took my sister and me to Christian Science Sunday School. My mother, who remained a student of Christian Science throughout her life, lived to age 101. As a mother myself and one who owes her life to Christian Science, I am grateful to be serving as a Christian Science practitioner today.

The sort of mother love or fostering care shown in the original adoption in this case crops up repeatedly in these testimonies and plays a large role in the records of children's healings. Even so sweeping a critic of Christian Science as Mark Twain could see that. One of the few things that impressed him deeply in the new faith was its actual healing results, which he not only praised but also related to the cures of the New Testament. With his characteristic blend of wild irony and common sense he struck out at those who would make it a crime for parents to rely on Christian Science rather than medical treatment for their children's health. A note in his boisterously polemic *Christian Science* makes this clear:

I have received several letters (two from educated and ostensibly intelligent persons), which contained, in substance, this protest: "I don't object to men and women chancing their lives with these people [Christian Scientists], but it is a burning shame that the law should allow them to trust their helpless little children in their deadly hands." Isn't it touching? Isn't it deep? Isn't it modest? It is as if the person said, "I know that to a parent his child is the core of his heart, the apple of his eye, a possession so dear, so precious that he will trust its life in no hands but those which he believes with all his soul to be the very best and the very safest, but it is a burning shame that the law does not require him to come to *me* to ask what kind of healer I will allow him to call." The public is merely a multiplied "me."[4]

BIRTH

Because most Western countries require that a physician or licensed midwife be employed in all cases of childbirth, this is one area of frequent and necessary cooperation between doctors and Christian Scientists. Many of the latter prefer to have home deliveries, and usually there is no difficulty in finding a doctor willing to cooperate in such a situation. Many other Christian Scientists find it more convenient to utilize hospital facilities for the actual birth. Both kinds of experience are represented in the affidavits in this section.

These accounts are introduced by a letter from a physician in a large metropolitan area to a Christian Science practitioner with whom he had personal contact. The letter was entirely voluntary. It has been slightly abridged to protect the identity of the writer and his hospital associates.

Letter from a physician to a Christian Science practitioner

June 5, 1981

Dear Mrs. _____ :

I am writing this letter as a medical practitioner who has had considerable experience in caring for the obstetrical needs of Christian Scientists in the _____ area. This experience has been unique and rewarding.

I have had the privilege of attending approximately 200 Christian Science births. This close association with people of this faith and the resultant exchange of ideas has provided me an opportunity to understand and appreciate their belief that man is constituted in God's image. . . .

It has been my fortunate experience to work with a number of Christian Science practitioners during the birth process, all of whom have accepted my efforts with flexible understanding and love, while still maintaining their faith and devotion to God's law. Our common ground is expressed in the phrase "We are working together for good." With this as a watch word I have yet to encounter a situation where conflict arose.

In the beginning I must admit there was apprehension by me as well as the hospital staff in regard to our Christian Science patients. This fear centered on imagined interference with our duties, a denial of our problems and possible legal entanglement. Our experience has been entirely contrary to these fears. Our Christian Science patients have at all times given careful consideration to our problems. In certain instances they have courteously declined, or legally waived, many examinations considered routine; thus they have taken upon themselves the responsibilities for these omissions. Their expression of gratitude toward the staff has gained the staff's understanding and devotion.

When medical action appeared necessary it was preceded by a calm and considerate discussion of the situation with both the patient and the practitioner. It was my constant observation that the practitioner urged the patient to exercise free choice and was then supportive of that choice. A sensitivity was maintained that each Christian Scientist demonstrates what he can to the best of his understanding. . . .

Frequently an interval of time was requested in which to work out the problem through Christian Science. Most frequently the situation then became resolved. Such demonstrations became so frequent that the delivery room staff regarded these patients as behaving in quite a special way. Often the usual rules did not apply. Not infrequently an arrested labor, not expected to terminate for hours, would advance to delivery in a few minutes after phone consultation between patient and practitioner.

As for myself, I truly believe that I have experienced the law of God in operation through Christian Science. On one memorable occasion I was presented with an irrefutable demonstration of the healing power of Christian Science. A student of Christian Science had been in active labor for several hours without adequate progress. On examination a shoulder was found to be presenting, making normal delivery impossible. This finding was confirmed by x-ray examination and a further admonition by the consulting radiologist that a vaginal delivery was clearly impossible. This situation was discussed with the patient, her husband, and over the phone with the practitioner. A recommendation for immediate delivery by Caesarean section was made. The family requested a few moments alone together for silent prayer, after which I was requested to do whatever I felt was necessary. As it would require a short time to prepare surgery for the operation the patient and her family used the time in prayerful application of the principles of Christian Science. Fifteen minutes later on the way to surgery the patient turned quietly to me and asked if I would please examine her again. Without question and with absolute certainty I knew that I would find the impossible; delivery had now become possible, and so it was. We barely had time to return the patient for a normal delivery. The radiologist reviewed his films when told of the outcome and presented textbook evidence to prove it was impossible.

This experience was a moving one to all who were involved. Not only to the patient, who was the recipient of a healing, but to those of us who were present with her it was evident that this was a spiritual experience.

During my association with Christian Scientists I have seen many demonstrations through faith in the principles discovered by Mrs. Eddy. We have had two infants cured of a severe newborn respiratory problem of a type usually rapidly fatal without vigorous medical treatment, in each instance we had x-ray evidence of the problem. The healing took place before active medical treatment could be instituted. Many lesser problems were likewise handled. In all instances there has been perfect harmony in our working relations and a mutual respect. Freedom of choice has always been allowed by the practitioner to the patients and a full realization that in Christian Science a demonstration was a very individual thing and subject to the limits of one's understanding. . . .

Last week when I attended a [school] play put on by the first, second, third, and fourth grades and saw so many of my "babies" performing it seemed very, very worthwhile.

Sincerely yours,
[Name withheld]

Affidavit of Susan J. Durnford, then of Brookline, Massachusetts, in 1980

I went into labor for the delivery of my first child on December 19, 1979. The birth took place in our home at 913 Ferry Street in Marshfield, Massachusetts. The labor was quite prolonged and without significant progress for some eighteen hours. The labor then ceased for a time and the physician in attendance, Dr. _____ of Brookline, Massachusetts, left, promising to return when there was some change. The two Christian Science nurses in attendance, Miss Elsie Van Der Geest and Miss Laurie Quiggen, also left.

I had engaged the services of a Christian Science practitioner for treatment through prayer during the birth. I spoke with her by telephone at this time, telling her that the labor was making no progress. Then I went to bed to rest. Within minutes labor began to build again and this time progressed normally. Dr. _____ and the two nurses returned several hours later and the baby was born healthy, normal, and strong.

When Dr. _____ examined the afterbirth, he discovered that the placenta had begun to separate prematurely, inducing the initial premature phase of labor, and then had sealed itself, enabling the birth to go on normally. I was informed by the doctor that a full separation of the placenta would have caused the baby to have been born dead from lack of oxygen. In a letter to me following the birth, Dr. _____ wrote: "I believe that faith, the work of the practitioner, and calmness of the patient averted the disaster."

Affidavit of Linda Ruffner-Russell of Otterville, Illinois, in 1981

That my son, Thomas Kristian Russell, was born on August 20, 1980, after a protracted period of labor, at _____ Hospital in _____, Illinois. I had been at the hospital in labor for over a day. The obstetrician on the case was Dr. A____. A second physician at the hospital, Dr. B____, examined the baby shortly after birth and found that the baby was having serious breathing problems.

Without our prior knowledge, Dr. B____ called in a specialist, Dr. C____. Dr. C____ diagnosed the infant's condition as pneumonia caused by the prolonged labor. When Dr. C____ informed me of Kristian's condition, he stated that the baby's lungs were inflamed and that if he were not sent by helicopter or ambulance to intensive care facilities in nearby Springfield, Illinois or St. Louis, Missouri, he would be dead by morning.

I explained to the doctor that I could not make this decision without first talking to my husband, Thomas Russell, who after staying in the hospital with me the full previous day, had left for home. Dr. C____ insisted again that the child must be sent immediately to an intensive care facility. I explained to him that I was a Christian Scientist and believed deeply in the power of prayer to heal even in the most difficult situations. At this point Dr. C____ left the case, stating that he would take no responsibility for the child if he were not immediately sent to Springfield or St. Louis.

My husband returned later that evening, and we decided not to have the baby transferred to the intensive care facility. I called the Christian Science practitioner who had prayed for me during the birth and asked her to continue to pray for the child. I prayed the entire night myself. In the morning the baby was examined again. The doctors reported his condition as considerably improved, though still critical. At this point Dr. C____ came back on the case. However, he laid out in detail what he considered to be the very serious dangers of the child's present condition. We agreed to have the child kept in an incubator at the doctor's request, but he was given no drugs or other treatment.

On the second day after the birth, Dr. C____ reported

that Kristian's condition continued to improve but said that the infant must have liquid nutriment. Since the doctor indicated that the baby could not be nursed, we gave permission for special tubes to be inserted for feeding through the nose.

On the third day Dr. C____ informed me that in spite of the marked improvement, Kristian was still in serious condition with only a 50-50 chance of survival. Dr. C____ stated that if the child were not given antibiotics it was unlikely that he would survive. I again explained my trust and conviction in the power of prayer to heal. He again expressed disapproval of our position but stayed on the case.

Until the third day my husband and I had not been permitted to touch or hold the child. At our request, however, we were given permission to hold the child for short periods. We also came to feel that Kristian's progress was not being accurately monitored. One nurse would report that he could not be taken out of the incubator for more than a few minutes, while another would leave him with me for a half hour. By the fourth day, we felt that it would be in the best interest of the child that he be nursed rather than fed through inserted tubes. On learning of this decision on our part, however, Dr. C____ abruptly quit the case.

This was a Sunday. No other doctor in the area was available who would consent to take the case. The hospital administrator, Mr. _____, was called in. My husband and I explained that we did not wish to take the baby from the hospital if this would cause alarm, but that we felt it would not be in the best interest of the child to remain so largely separated from his parents or to be fed through tubes.

The administrator himself then called Dr. C____ by phone and asked him if he would be willing to take the case again. Dr. C____ agreed. Mr. _____ told us that Dr. C____ had termed Kristian's progress thus far "miraculous," but that he was still concerned about the child's condition. We therefore gave permission for the feeding tubes to be used one more day if the doctor felt this to be absolutely necessary. But when Dr. C____ examined him the next day, he reported that the tubes would not be needed. From that point on the child was fed normally.

I was in touch with the practitioner continually throughout

the week after the birth. Although officially released from the hospital myself, I remained there in order to be with the child. Throughout this week I was informed by Dr. C____ that the period of recovery Kristian would require would be quite lengthy. On the eighth day after the birth, however, Dr. C____ came in and told me that my son was in perfect condition and that I could take him home.

In 1985 the child's father, a juvenile court judge in Illinois, recapitulated this episode in a thoughtful letter to the National Center on Child Abuse in Washington, D.C.

Letter from Thomas Gilbert Russell to the National Center on Child Abuse, June 10, 1985

. . . Let me share one experience, among many, from my personal experience which supports the rationale of these suggestions.

At the time of the birth of our son in a local hospital the prognosis was that he would not survive the night unless he was transferred immediately to a special intensive infant care unit at a hospital eighty miles away. As Christian Scientists my wife and I declined to authorize the transfer, indicating our desire to rely entirely on our form of spiritual healing. A Christian Science practitioner was engaged to assist us through prayer. While there was evidence of improvement the next morning, it was strongly urged that antibiotics be administered. Again we gently declined. Over a period of eight days every dire medical prognostication was reversed and on the eighth day the child was pronounced to be in perfect health and ordered released. He is now a happy, intelligent four-year-old. After such an experience I could not be persuaded that the method we chose was at all inferior to the medical alternatives available to us. The pediatrician in attendance even conceded that the remarkable change in the baby's condition could be attributable to nothing but the method of healing we employed. . . .

Affidavit of Mary Gottschalk of Wellesley, Massachusetts, in 1986

The day after my son Laird was born I was told he had a broken collar bone. The delivery took place at 6:20 p.m. on April

25, 1970, at Bryn Mawr Hospital in Bryn Mawr, Pennsylvania. Dr. Nelson Matthews was the obstetrician. Laird weighed over ten pounds at birth and had unusually broad shoulders for an infant. The doctors stated they believed the bone had snapped during the delivery and said the break was visible without an X-ray.

Although I had held Laird immediately following the delivery, hospital policy dictated that all newborns be kept in a "hot box" for twenty-four hours and that they be examined by a pediatrician named by the parents. Dr. Matthews had recommended Dr. Charles H. Classen, the head pediatrician of the hospital. The week prior to delivery I phoned Dr. Classen, asking permission to use his name as pediatrician at the hospital, and mentioning that I am a Christian Scientist. Our first meeting took place when he entered my room late on the morning of April 26. His first words were, "I'm glad you're a Christian Scientist." He explained the nature of the severe fracture he had found on examining the child, and that the medical-surgical route would involve setting the bone and possible corrective surgery, a brace or a body cast, and a period in traction of six to eighteen months. Dr. Classen asked me—much to my surprise—if I would be willing to take the responsibility to trust the case to Christian Science.

I had been supported and strengthened through the prayer of a Christian Science practitioner prior to and through the delivery. I also felt very clearly that God cares for each of us completely, no matter what the evidence to the senses is. So it was natural to feel a real sense of joy without any burden in accepting the responsibility. I agreed to stay with the child at the hospital so he could be checked the next day. I explained the circumstances to the practitioner and asked her to pray for the child. I spent much of the rest of the day in prayer myself. To my surprise again, a nurse brought Laird to me before the twenty-four [hour] period was over, and I was able to nurse him quite peacefully.

On the morning of April 27, Dr. Classen examined Laird again and said we could go home. He showed me a tiny bump under the skin over the collarbone where he said the bone had set and knit perfectly. He suggested only that I use front-closing shirts and put his left arm into his clothes first when dressing him in order to avoid strain on that part of the shoulder. The healing was further confirmed six weeks later when I went for examination to Dr. Matthews at his request. He asked about the break and examined the baby for any effect or trace of it. The tiny bump was gone, and he agreed that it was completely healed. There have been no aftereffects. Laird has participated in many demanding physical activities including sports since he was small, and has always had full and unrestricted use of his arms.

Affidavit of Betty Louise Brunn of Scottsdale, Arizona, in 1980

When my youngest son, John Norse, was born in November 1946, my husband was stationed at the naval base in Charleston, South Carolina, and we were living nearby. The child arrived six weeks prematurely. His feet were visibly malformed, but I assumed this to be the result of the premature delivery and a condition that would heal as the child grew.

When John was three months old, I took him, in compliance with Navy regulations, to the medical facility on base for the first of a series of immunization shots. The Navy physician who administered the shot examined him and, after taking X-rays, informed me that the child was double club-footed and that one heel, due to a congenital deformity, had no joint whatsoever. He said the child would never be able to walk.

The doctor indicated that the boy's feet could be straightened only by putting them in a cast for a period of months, and that the bone deformity in the heel could not be corrected at all. He stated that when the boy got older, the foot should be amputated and the boy given an artificial foot.

I learned later from my husband that the physician who had delivered the child, Admiral _____, had informed him of the clubfoot condition at the time of the birth. My husband said that in their concern for my own condition after the difficult birth, they had decided not to break the news to me at that time.

As a lifelong Christian Scientist I had witnessed the healing of many physical ailments and could not accept the doctor's prognosis as final. I told the doctor that I would rely on Christian Science for the healing and, with the permission of the boy's father, engaged a Christian Science practitioner to pray for the child. When I took the child back to the base hospital for the next shot four weeks after the first, the same Navy doctor who had diagnosed the condition informed me that the feet had straightened by 15°. When I took the child for the third required shot after another month, this doctor told me that the feet had straightened another 40°. He stated that he could not explain the change, since the feet had not been placed in a corrective cast, but that I should keep up whatever I was doing for the child. He still indicated, however, that the boy would never be able to bend or use normally the one foot that had no heel joint, and that the boy would have difficulties even in standing.

John learned to walk, though at first very pigeon-toed, by the time he was fifteen months. When he stumbled and fell, his brother and sisters would pick him up. I continued, all during this period, to pray for the complete healing, and the child's activities became increasingly less impaired.

The family moved to Pearl Harbor when my husband was transferred there in 1948, and it was there that the complete healing was confirmed. One day when John was three years old, he and a friend were found missing from home. After some searching by the local police and Naval MP's, the two were located inside the base at Pearl Harbor, looking at the ships. The boy's father, concerned because the child had walked so far, had him examined by the doctors on base. They found no indication of anything wrong with his feet.

When the boy was 10, he became a catcher on the Little League baseball team, and many times I went—not to watch the baseball game, really—but to express my gratitude for his absolute freedom from all that had been predicted. He later entered the Air Force, undergoing and passing a complete physical examination. His activities have been entirely unimpaired.

The following personal testimony by William Randolph Hearst appeared in his syndicated column "In the News" (July 17, 1941) and was later reprinted by him in a brochure entitled "Faith." It is included here as an example of a healing in a much publicized family whose members never became Christian Scientists. Though written in Hearst's unique style of popular journalism, it represents a not unusual phenomenon: a healing through Christian Science accepted gratefully by the recipients but not leading to any further commitment. This phenomenon, it may be noted, has New Testament parallels.

"Most people have had occurrences which might be termed miracles in their own families," wrote Hearst. "Your columnist witnessed such a spiritual translation, such an entirely unmaterial healing, such a miraculous rescue of his own son from the very jaws of death." In his column Hearst recounted the story of a son born with a closed pylorus, the sphincter that connects the stomach with the bowel. This condition made it impossible for the child to retain even a teaspoonful of milk, and without such nourishment, he lost weight, grew alarmingly weak, and hovered near death. The doctors who had been summoned recommended surgery, but they had no confidence that the baby had the strength even to survive the operation that might repair his condition.

One evening, during this critical period, a friend of the Hearst family brought a Christian Science practitioner to their home. "Your columnist is not a Christian Scientist," Hearst reported, "but he turned in desperation to this gleam of hope." That night, the practitioner prayed over the child and by morning he was able to take some milk, retain it, and begin his recovery. That child, Hearst reported in 1941, was now six feet tall and ran a newspaper "considerably better than his father can."

When he was asked why he never became a Christian Scientist himself, Hearst said that it wasn't as easy for him to change his thinking as it would be for a child. "You know, folks," he explained, "children are the best patients for spiritual healing. . . . They have no preconceived erroneous convictions—no false beliefs that have to be overcome before the truth can enter their consciousness."

In a letter to a Christian Scientist on February 27, 1979, William Randolph Hearst, Jr. (who had been the baby in question) corroborated that this was the way he had always heard the story from his father and mother. The Christian Science practitioner who was called in, he added, had been recommended to his father by one of the latter's editors, Merrill Goddard. The only correction he would have made in the elder Hearst's somewhat florid account was, he remarked, one not of fact but of judgment. "I'm afraid," he wrote wryly, "that neither

Pop nor I ever knew the day when I could run a newspaper better than he."

YOUTH

The evidence of innumerable testimonies suggests that children respond even more readily than adults to Christian Science treatment. Mrs. Eddy writes in *Science and Health:* "Laboring long to shake the adult's faith in matter and to inculcate a grain of faith in God,—an inkling of the ability of Spirit to make the body harmonious,—the author has often remembered our Master's love for little children, and understood how truly such as they belong to the heavenly kingdom."[5] Very often, however, a child's healing involves also a healing of the parents' fears.

The testimonies in this section all have to do with children or teenagers.

Affidavit of Mrs. Dusenbury of Chicago, Illinois, in March 1982

Mrs. Patricia G. Dusenbury, being first duly sworn, deposes and says

That as an infant, our son . . . was sickly and frequently under medical care. In February, 19___, when he was about ___ months old, he came down with croup and had great difficulty breathing. We took him to Maine General Hospital in Portland, Maine, where he remained under treatment for two weeks. He proved allergic to the drugs initially used, which caused a violent reaction. The doctors at the hospital finally diagnosed his problem as hypogammaglobulinemia and stated that he would require massive regular injections of gamma globulin. The condition, according to the physicians, rendered him extremely susceptible to upper respiratory infection.

Our family physician, Dr. A___ of Portland, Maine, administered these injections in the months after [our son's] release from the hospital. The general pattern of ill health continued, however, and the child came down with pneumonia the next winter. Dr. A___ stated at that point that there was little he could do beyond keeping the child alive, and advised us to move to a drier climate if possible. He stated that he doubted [our son] would live through another winter if we remained in New England.

The family moved to Phoenix, Arizona, in the summer of 1959. The move did not lessen our child's constant sicknesses. He was under the care of a prominent pediatrician in the area, a Dr. B____, during this time, and we continued to take [our son] every few weeks for the prescribed injections of gamma globulin. This went on for more than five years. The dosage level was gradually increased, however, and the drug began to produce adverse mental side effects—nightmares, from which we were sometimes unable to awaken our son except by cold shower.

My husband and I finally decided to stop altogether the program that the doctors had instituted for our child. This was at the time that I earnestly started to study and apply the teachings of Christian Science.

One Wednesday afternoon shortly after we had made this decision, our son became ill with a high temperature and severe earache. I gathered up the Bible and *Science and Health with Key to the Scriptures* by Mary Baker Eddy and sat by the youngster's bedside in prayer. In a short while he fell asleep and his temperature dropped closer to normal. As I began preparing dinner for the family, I continued my prayer, applying what I'd learned from the study of Christian Science.

Although the pain was dispelled, the child was still not well by the time of the regular Wednesday evening testimony meeting at the local Christian Science church. My husband assured me he would care for our son while I went to the meeting, but I was torn between a desire to stay at home with the child and my own deep need for the spiritual inspiration I had found at these meetings in the past.

Rather reluctantly I went on to church. The very first testifier was a mother who related a healing of her own child. The woman stated that even though it had not been possible for her to reach home immediately after being informed of the youngster's condition, she knew that God was right there caring for the child. Her prayer, she said, lifted her fear. The testifier indicated that when she did return home she found the youngster completely healed.

That testimony gave me a conviction that our son, too, was

in God's care whether or not I was personally present with him. I found myself reaching out in silent prayer with a sense of assurance that the boy was healed. By the time I returned home that evening, his ear had drained and he was completely well. This healing took place in February or March, 1964, and it has remained permanent. It marked the end of the sickliness and constant attacks of respiratory infection. He rarely even had colds in his subsequent childhood years. The nightmares also ceased. I joined the Church of Christ, Scientist, not long after that time, and have both experienced and witnessed many other healings through prayer in Christian Science.

Mrs. Dusenbury's account was supported by a brief affidavit from her husband.

Affidavit of Liph S. Dusenbury in March 1982

Liph S. Dusenbury, being first duly sworn, deposes and says:

That I can attest to the healing of our son . . . of hypogammaglobulinemia, as described in the accompanying affidavit of my wife, Patricia G. Dusenbury. Although I am not a Christian Scientist myself, I attribute this healing to the results of prayer.

Notarized statement of Walter Studer of Winterthur, Switzerland, in January 1983

Our daughter was nine years old when our family spent some vacation days in a tent by Lake Constance. This was in 1956. Because of poor weather we soon returned home to Weinfelden. Both our children became seriously ill. Our eight-year-old son was soon well. However, our little daughter continued to grow worse.

We were Christian Scientists at the time, but still quite new in our study of it. Since the child had to stay away from school because of the illness, we were required to call a doctor. The doctor we reached, Dr. A ___ of _____, diagnosed a serious case of diphtheria. He came to our house twice daily for approximately two weeks to monitor the child's condition and give her a daily injection of penicillin. Almost every day he expressed new fears for the child's life and our fear also grew until it seemed insurmountable. After a bad attack one day, in which the child lost consciousness, we decided to dismiss the doctor and turn for healing to Christian Science.

The following day I went to Dr. A___ to tell him of my decision. I had to sign a paper releasing him from any responsibility. The very same day I went to the district school physician, Dr. B___ of _____, as I felt I was required to let him also be aware of our decision. Dr. B___ told me our daughter's condition was very serious. His examination confirmed the diagnosis of diphtheria and also revealed that she had developed penicillin poisoning through the medication given her. He said there was little hope that if [she lived] she would become normal again. Perhaps because the medical prognosis was so bleak, he voiced no objection to our turning to Christian Science.

We asked a friend, an experienced Christian Scientist, to pray for the child. Several days later someone called our attention to a children's home not far away run by Christian Scientists. We immediately telephoned the home and after a few days were able to place the child there. With continued Christian Science help, her condition stabilized and began to improve.

Over the next weeks we filled our thought with a better understanding of God. We read the *Herald of Christian Science,* sang hymns from the *Christian Science Hymnal,* and daily studied the Bible lesson in the *Christian Science Quarterly.* Within about a month, she was able to walk, talk, and see again. Dr. B had suggested that the condition would leave her permanently cross-eyed, but there were no such aftereffects. Five weeks from the time she entered the children's home we were able to take her home to Weinfelden, completely healed.

The full healing was confirmed by Dr. B___, who examined her prior to her return to school. He said that a miracle had happened. Today our daughter, _____, is the mother of a ten-year-old son. This healing inspired me to dedicate my own efforts to the healing work of Christian Science, and I have since become a Christian Science practitioner.

Affidavit of Kathryn Ashby, now of Anchorage, Alaska, in 1980

My son, Roderick Schenker, was struck by a car while walking across a highway in May 1974. We were living in Juneau, Alaska, at the time. Roddy was five years old. I was telephoned by the manager of the apartment complex in which we were living, who told me the child had been taken to the hospital in an ambulance. I called a Christian Science practitioner, who agreed to give the child prayerful treatment, and I then drove to Bartlett Memorial Hospital where Roddy had been taken. The medical diagnosis of my son's injuries included a concussion— the result of a deep gash on the head—and broken bones in the shoulder. Roddy had been conscious on and off in the ambulance, and was conscious when I arrived in the hospital emergency room. He told me then that he wanted to trust God to heal him.

I requested the right to rely wholly on Christian Science for the care of the child. Initially, I was permitted to take the child home, but because of the great concern expressed by the physician and others about the child's condition, we were required to bring the child back to the hospital for X-rays and further examination. The X-rays, taken the night of the accident, showed multiple fractures of the shoulder. Dr. Willard Andrews, the physician who made the examination, showed me the X-rays and pointed out the fractures specifically. I thanked him for his concern, but asked that we be allowed to continue to rely on Christian Science treatment. I felt that this was the best form of care that any child could possibly have. In bringing up my own seven children, we had experienced many, many healings of a wide range of conditions, including the setting of broken bones through prayer. By the time the X-ray was taken, incidentally, the gash in the child's head had closed up considerably, though no stitches had been taken or medication given.

We took Roddy home again after a simple cloth sling was put on him to make the arm and shoulder comfortable. The next day Roddy spent quietly in our home, but the following day he was out playing with limited use of his arm. During the next week the members of our family companioned in prayer for this child. The practitioner also continued Christian Science treatment.

A few days after the accident, I received a letter from Dr. Andrews describing Roddy's injuries in detail and stating that in the Doctor's opinion the shoulder needed to be set surgically. But the progress toward healing had already been made. In fact, in about two weeks Roddy was completely healed. His

Sunday School teacher called me the next Sunday to report that Roddy had been lifting both his arms high above his head and swinging them all around before class started, elatedly exclaiming to a fellow pupil, "Look, Timmy, at what I can do!" Roddy has had full use of his arms since that time, playing basketball and baseball, and has experienced no aftereffects from the accident whatsoever.

Affidavit of Ellen Hamilton, now of Heartland, Wisconsin, in March 1980

On September 16, 1979, my husband, son, and daughter were scalded when a boiler blew up. My husband . . . received first and second degree burns over 15 per cent of his body, and our daughter, Kristen, then four years old, received third degree burns over the left foot and ankle and right heel. My son was injured less seriously.

My husband is not a Christian Scientist, and all three were taken to _____ Burn Center in Milwaukee. My husband remained there for two weeks before coming home to recuperate. Kristen was bandaged and permitted to go home after a few hours. We returned to the Burn Center every other day for the next two weeks to have the bandages changed. Because of the child's resistance to having the bandages changed, she was given a drug to quiet her on each of these occasions.

During this period, Kristen was under the care of one of the burn experts at the Center, Dr. _____. The doctor stated that the healing would take months. He indicated initially that the burn would probably not result in a permanent scar, but when the condition showed little or no improvement after two weeks, he informed us that a scar was likely, that a lengthy course of further medical treatment was necessary, and that the child might permanently drag the foot because of damage to the tendons in her ankle. He also stated that the symptoms of impetigo were evident on the damaged skin.

It was at this point that I placed the child wholly under Christian Science care. I asked a Christian Science practitioner to give the child treatment through prayer and called the Christian Science nurse, Mrs. Polly Kerr, for proper care in changing the bandages and cleansing the damaged skin. Within three days, the condition of the foot and ankle was visibly improved.

The nurse visited the home on one occasion, and subsequently we took the child to Clearview Sanatorium, a Christian Science care facility in Delafield, Wisconsin, to have the bandages changed there. No further medication was given, and the child no longer resisted having the bandages changed.

In less than three weeks from the time of our turning to Christian Science treatment and care, the burn was completely covered with fresh skin. There was no further need for a bandage, and the visible signs of the burn were fading. Kristen was back in her kindergarten class shortly thereafter. She favored her foot in walking for a brief period, but Christian Science treatment was continued, and she now walks and runs normally.

Mrs. Hamilton's account was supported in further detail by an affidavit by the attending Christian Science nurse, whose report throws an interesting light on the nature of Christian Science nursing care and the question of child neglect.

Affidavit of Polly Kerr (now Simonsen) of Brookfield, Wisconsin, in March 1980

I am a Christian Science nurse employed by the Clearview Sanatorium, a Christian Science care facility in Delafield, Wisconsin.

On October 1, 1979, I was called to change the bandages of Kristen Hamilton, the daughter of Mr. and Mrs. Hamilton, of Greendale, Wisconsin, while the child was under Christian Science treatment for third degree burns on her left foot and ankle and the heel of her right foot. The child had been under medical care at _____ Burn Center in Milwaukee for the two previous weeks.

I went to the Hamilton home on October 2 to change the bandages. The following day I received a telephone call from Dr. _____ of _____ Burn Center, who informed me that because the child was no longer being brought for treatment and care at the Burn Center or other medical facility, he intended to refer the case to County officials under child neglect statutes. He stated that he would suggest to these officials that the child be taken under protective custody in order for medical treatment to be continued.

The doctor described at length and in detail the severity and nature of the burns. He stated that the skin would possibly never heal even under the best of conditions and that he expected a large scar to remain unless new skin were grafted onto the burned area. He stated that the only way the flesh could possibly fill in was from the edges and that this process, if it took place at all, would be extremely slow and extend over a period of three months or more. He stated that because of damage to the tendons in the child's ankle, she would possibly never walk normally.

The doctor then asked what specific steps were being taken to care for the burns. I explained that the child was being given Christian Science treatment through prayer and explained my own role as a Christian Science nurse in the bandaging and cleansing of the burn. I related to him step by step the bandaging procedures used in my first visit to the home the previous day. I identified the cleansing agent and specific dressing materials used. When I had explained to Dr. _____ the nature of the care being given the child, he reversed his previous position and stated that he was satisfied that the child was receiving adequate physical care. He then indicated that he no longer intended to refer the case to County authorities. He asked me to report to him in two weeks, however, on the condition of the wound.

Mrs. Hamilton continued to bring Kristen to Clearview Sanatorium periodically for the cleansing and rebandaging of the wound for three weeks. The condition was healing visibly during this time. When I called Dr. _____ after two weeks to report on the child's condition, new growth was already covering much of the burned area. By October 24, one week later, the wound was completely closed. New skin had grown in to cover the burned area completely, and the physical signs of the burn were fading. There was no scar, and no further need for bandaging.

Affidavit of William B. Forney of Glenwood, Georgia, in February 1980

In May, 1945, my son . . . came down with a disease that was diagnosed as spinal meningitis. He was eleven months old at the time. We were living in Louisville, Georgia. I had left on a business trip to Augusta, Georgia, on Thursday morning and that night my wife . . . called to tell me that the child was ill. She had called a local physician, Dr. _____, who came to the house.

My wife was not then a Christian Scientist, but I had been a Christian Scientist all my life and prayed to lift my own fear for the child. My wife informed me by telephone the following day that the boy was still having medical treatment, but that his condition had not improved. When I arrived home on Saturday night, the child's condition had deteriorated greatly. Dr. _____ was there at the house. He informed me then that [my son] had spinal meningitis, and that he did not expect the boy to live through the night.

Dr. _____ had been in consultation with a Dr. _____ of University Hospital in Augusta, and wanted to take the child to University Hospital that night. Since my own car was being repaired at the time, he offered to drive us to Augusta himself, and we agreed.

While the doctor was making arrangements for the trip, my wife and I talked the matter over. I told her that I would stand by her decision, whether she chose to rely on medical treatment or to turn to Christian Science, and that she should be comfortable in the decision whatever it was. At this point she decided to turn to Christian Science. I called Dr. _____, explained our decision to him, and thanked him for his concern and help. I asked that he send us a bill for his services. I then called my mother, Mrs. Bertha Forney, a Christian Science practitioner in Augusta and asked for Christian Science treatment through prayer for the child. By the next morning, a Sunday, the child's condition had markedly improved. And by Monday the boy was completely well.

Many townspeople in Louisville heard of this healing and commented to me about it. My wife became a Christian Scientist shortly after this time and our family has had many healings through reliance on Christian Science over the years. My son . . . is healthy and active today. . . .

Affidavit of Patricia Lamb Turbeville of Pittsburgh, Pennsylvania, in October 1981

I was struck by polio in 1943 when I was 16. We were living in Rocky River, Ohio, and I had just started my junior year at

Rocky River High School. My mother, Mrs. Alice Lamb, cared for me in the initial stages of the disease. She then took me to be examined by doctors in Cleveland, who, after a thorough examination, diagnosed the condition as poliomyelitis.

Although my parents were not members of the Christian Science Church at the time, I had attended Christian Science Sunday School and my grandmother, Mrs. Freda S. Lamb, was a Christian Science practitioner. My mother asked me whether I wanted to have medical treatment or to rely on Christian Science. I decided to rely on Christian Science, and we asked my grandmother for help through prayer. I went to stay with her and my grandfather at their home in Kewaunee, Wisconsin, for the next several months. By the time I returned for Thanksgiving my condition had improved considerably, though I walked with difficulty and was still unable to use one arm.

When I returned to Rocky River, we asked a local Christian Science practitioner for continued help through prayer. I took a bus and streetcar once each week to see her. I missed about six months of school altogether, but gradually regained the full use of my legs and arms. I returned to school in time to finish my junior year with my class. I was able to play a role that spring in a musical production of "HMS Pinafore" and in the following summer to attend a music camp in the Adirondacks. By that time I was completely healed.

The healing has been permanent and left no aftereffects. I have no handicaps today and am in good health. I have led an active life, raised a family, and continued the study of Christian Science through the years.

Mrs. Turbeville's account is supported by the following affidavit by her mother.

Affidavit of Mrs. Alice D. Lamb of St. Simon Island, Georgia, in 1981

The circumstances that brought me into Christian Science occurred when our eldest daughter, Patricia, was suffering from polio. This was in 1943, shortly after Pat had started her junior year of high school. Our family was then living in Rocky River, Ohio, where we had recently moved. At the time I was not a member of the Christian Science Church, though I knew something of Christian Science through my husband's mother, who was a Christian Science practitioner. My husband had also been healed earlier of a serious back injury through Christian Science.

When Patricia, then 16, came down with the disease, my husband was away on a business trip. Applying what I knew of Christian Science, I prayed for her and nursed her through the fever at home until it subsided. When it became apparent that Patricia's condition was not improving and that she had possibly suffered an attack of polio, however, I took her to a doctor in Cleveland recommended by my husband's business associate as one of the outstanding physicians in the area.

The physician, Dr. Harley Williams, was associated with Western Reserve University. After examining Patricia, he called in two other physicians, including a Dr. Harbin, a polio specialist. Patricia was then given a further thorough examination. The doctors informed me that Patricia was indeed suffering from poliomyelitis. Dr. Williams told me that she had been well cared for and could have been in far worse condition given the severity of the case, but that she would nevertheless be crippled for life. He stated that her condition was not contagious or a danger to others, but that she should be placed in a hospital for a long period and spend the remainder of her days strapped in a back brace to keep her spine from curving.

When I told the doctors we were considering Christian Science treatment, they indicated that this might be good if it would give her comfort and peace of mind, but that the damage done to her body was incurable and no therapy could restore her to full health. As we were leaving Dr. Williams' office, he remarked that he would have to register our daughter's case with the city health department.

On the way home I asked Patricia which means of treatment she preferred. She stated that she would prefer to rely on Christian Science. Shortly thereafter we sent Patricia to stay with my husband's parents in Kewaunee, Wisconsin. We asked my husband's mother, Mrs. Freda S. Lamb, for Christian Science help through prayer. She cared for Patricia in their home over the next several months. When Patricia returned at Thanksgiving time, 1943, her condition was considerably improved, though she was still unable to use one of her arms and dragged both legs in walking.

We called a local Christian Science practitioner for further help through prayer, and Patricia visited her each week over the next few months. Her condition continued to improve, and Patricia was able to return to school in time to finish her junior year. That spring she was asked to play the lead role in her high school production of "HMS Pinafore" and was able to do so, both dancing and singing. By the end of the school year, she had regained full use of her arms and legs.

The healing has been complete in every way. I realized this myself when I went with Patricia and some of her friends on a canoe trip in the Adirondacks in the summer after her junior year. There I saw her take part in all the activities of the trip without restriction. The healing led me to take up the study of Christian Science seriously, and I later joined the church. Patricia did also. She now has four grown children of her own.

Declaration by Margaret Elizabeth Lees of Great Barr, Birmingham, West Midlands, England, in January 1983

In September 1938 when I was a month short of my thirteenth birthday, and living at Lindfield in Sussex, I was afflicted with polio during a local polio epidemic. I was taken to Haywards Heath Hospital and remained there in isolation, during the acute stage of the illness, thereafter in a general ward, for an initial period of six weeks. Then I went home for three days, but it was decided that only a hospital could provide the environment for the necessary intensive muscular therapy that I required, and I returned to Haywards Heath Hospital where I remained until May 1939.

The family's doctor who attended me at this time, and was also in charge of my case in hospital, was Dr. Whitfield of a local partnership, the name of which I believe I recall correctly was Whitfield, Mather, and Todd.

The calf of my left leg was 1¾" less in diameter than that of my right. There was some improvement during my time in hospital. When in due course the condition of the leg was stabilised, no further improvement was taking place, and I was told that there would be permanent disability, I was sent home. I immediately returned to school, but could not move any distance without leaning on an arm and had to be carried upstairs. My left leg collapsed when any weight was put upon it, and it was still visibly wasted compared with the other leg.

Three weeks after returning home and going back to school, that is to say at the end of May, my mother heard about Christian Science, of which we had no prior knowledge, from her sister-in-law in America with whom she had been in touch about my condition. My aunt gave us the address of the nearest Christian Science services which we went to, and of a neighbouring Christian Science practitioner whom my mother and I visited and who began to pray for me. I remember long conversations with this practitioner, and that I was hungry for answers to my questions on how God healed. From the first I was able to accept the teachings of Christian Science and I found that even as a young girl it appealed to me as a logical faith.

There was immediate improvement. By the end of August there was no trace of the lameness, and the leg had returned to its normal appearance. I had not been receiving medical therapy of any kind after returning home. I cannot specifically pinpoint any one time at which my healing came, but the improvement took place over a period of ten weeks or so, and at the end of that time I had no difficulty in traveling daily to the Gregg Commercial College in Brighton fifteen miles from home, at which I had commenced studies after leaving school three days before the war began, walking half a mile from the station to the college and negotiating the stairs several times a day.

I might add that in June of that year, immediately after my return to school, I took an entrance exam for the college and passed, but because the family business had fallen on hard times we had no money to take up the place. We were so overjoyed with the physical healing that was going on that my mother and I had no doubt that our prayers would also be answered to enable me to go to the college, and in the most marvellous and unforseeable ways the necessary means were found.

Throughout the years since, this healing has been the greatest inspiration to me.

Affidavit of Mrs. Kathryn Ann Schmitt of Garden City, Michigan, in February 1980

I learned of Christian Science while in _____ Hospital in Detroit, Michigan, suffering with what was later diagnosed as multiple sclerosis. I had suddenly become ill in May, 1963, when a senior at Mackenzie High School. My parents took me to the hospital, greatly alarmed at my condition. The doctors there were unable to diagnose the illness; they indicated, at one point, a possible brain tumor. I can remember praying, at a time when my condition seemed at its lowest ebb, not merely to be released from this physical illness but to understand more of what God is.

One of my fellow students, hearing of my condition, visited me in the hospital almost every day for the three weeks until I was released. He was a Christian Scientist; he later became my husband. During his visits, we talked a great deal about God. My friend did not refer particularly to Christian Science during these visits, but before I left the hospital he gave me a copy of *Science and Health with Key to the Scriptures.* I began to attend the Christian Science Sunday School shortly thereafter.

In January, 1964, I became ill again. My parents insisted on taking me to the _____ Hospital in _____, Michigan, this time where I stayed for some ten days. After extensive examination, the physician on my case, Dr. _____, informed my parents and me that I had multiple sclerosis. Dr. _____ told me that this was the same condition I had had the previous May at [the other hospital]. He told me that attacks of the disease would come at closer intervals in the future, that I could eventually become crippled, lose my speech, and suffer other physical consequences from the disease, which could eventually take my life.

When he explained the expected dire consequences of the disease, I told him simply that I would not accept the medical verdict or further medical treatment. From my brief contact with Christian Science, I had already gained a deep conviction that suffering is not God's will for man; and I was convinced that God's power can and does heal. I realized later that this conviction brought the healing. On the day following my conversation with Dr. _____, much to his surprise, the symptoms of the disease disappeared. The healing has been permanent, and I have experienced none of the effects predicted.

I took up the study of Christian Science in earnest in subsequent years. We have had many further healings over the years, and my husband and I regard it as a great privilege to raise our two sons as Christian Scientists.

Affidavit of Dorathea Wallworth of Gladwyne, Pennsylvania, in January 1980

In the summer of 1936 our daughter . . . , who was then five years old, became alarmingly ill. Despite prayerful work by a consecrated Christian Science practitioner, the condition was not healed immediately, and my husband, who was not a Christian Scientist, called a medical doctor, who in turn called two child specialists. They took her to Delaware County Hospital and said she had a rare disease called stretococci meningitis, for which they had no cure, and that they never had known a child to survive such an ordeal.

One of the specialists gently said to me, "I know you love your little girl, but because you do you must brace yourself to give her up, for if by some miracle she should live, we do not know how she would be affected. She might never walk; or she might be affected mentally."

All this time my mother and the faithful practitioner stood steadfastly by me. My husband and I prayed as we had never prayed before. One day, sitting in the hospital room, I was overcome with a sense of helplessness. The child's condition had not improved under medical treatment. But as I prayed to know that the child was truly in God's care, I was suddenly released from fear and discouragement. Even when one of the doctors said, "She isn't any worse, but don't get your hopes up for she can't possibly live," I was not impressed or discouraged nor did I doubt it.

At the end of two weeks, after much prayer on my part, my husband decided to turn wholly to Christian Science for the treatment of the child. He picked her up and carried her home from the hospital. No further medication was given. Shortly thereafter, with continued Christian Science treatment, she was completely healed. There was no period of convalescence and there were no aftereffects. Three weeks after she entered the hospital she attended a family wedding.

She later married and had three children, who attended the Christian Science Sunday School. Today they are still active church members.

We have had many healings in our family of all kinds of physical ills and inharmonious situations. But this is the one healing my thoughts always turn to when I want to express deepest gratitude, when some problem does not seem to yield as quickly or as completely as it should, or when I'm tempted to become fearful or discouraged about some experience. I am filled with the deepest and most humble gratitude to God for His tender loving care of my family and me through all these years.

Affidavit of Vance M. Patterson, now of Columbia, South Carolina, in 1982

In January 1969 I became ill and was taken to Newby Hospital, the infirmary at Hanover College in Hanover, Indiana. I was a freshman at the college at the time. I entered the infirmary on Thursday of "rush" week and found myself increasingly ill during the day. The doctor at the infirmary took blood tests and diagnosed the condition as acute rheumatic fever. He had to leave town the next morning, so another doctor was assigned to the case. After reviewing the tests, the second physician also informed me that I had contracted rheumatic fever. Both doctors stated that I would be in bed for at least 10–14 weeks.

Having attended the Christian Science Sunday School and relied on prayer for healing throughout my life, I decided to handle the condition entirely with Christian Science help. Speaking with my parents by telephone, I asked my mother to call a Christian Science practitioner for treatment through prayer. The nurses at the infirmary made me as comfortable as possible. I later spoke long-distance with the practitioner myself and spent as much time as I could in prayer and study of the Christian Science Bible Lesson. And by Friday afternoon I began to feel considerable relief from the pain.

The doctor at the infirmary indicated that I would be permitted to return to classes only after further blood tests gave indication of my recovery. The best place for me was at home, so they came Saturday morning and we flew home to Greentown, Indiana. Three days after arriving I was strong enough to get up and around, at first with crutches and after a few more days completely unaided. I went to see a local physician, Dr. _____, who had received the full records as to the tests at Newby Hospital and my diagnosed condition. When I strolled into his office the first thing he said was, "This boy ought to be in bed." He took more tests and prescribed that I take 12–15 aspirin per day. These were neither purchased nor taken, as I chose to continue relying wholly on prayer in Christian Science.

I spoke with the Christian Science practitioner regularly by phone during this period. After the third day home I was no longer confined to bed and was able to move freely with little pain. In another three or four days, with continued Christian Science treatment, I was completely free of pain. When we went to see Dr. _____ again a week or so after the first visit, he stated that no one could recover from rheumatic fever in such a short period and urged that I remain home longer. However, I was by then back to normal strength and experiencing no symptoms of the condition whatever. After waiting a few more days, I returned to school completely well.

The whole episode, from the start of the illness to my return to classes, took three weeks. The rheumatic fever had kept me completely confined in bed for only six days, and my full recovery had taken about ten days. A medical examination and further blood tests at the college infirmary several weeks after my return confirmed the healing. I have never been hampered in any way by side effects or had any form of relapse.

Mr. Patterson's account is supported and amplified by a further affidavit by his mother.

Affidavit of Martha M. Patterson of Columbia, South Carolina, in April 1982

In January 1969 we received a call from the Hanover College Infirmary to inform us that our son Vance was a patient there and had acute rheumatic fever. The examining physician said that he knew we would want to bring Vance home as he would need to be confined to bed for several months. He also stated that Vance must be moved by ambulance, as he was unable to sit in a car. We lived, at that time, in Greentown, Indiana, about one hundred miles from Hanover, and my husband, G. V. Patterson, arranged for his company's pilot and plane (which had a bed) to fly us down and Vance back the next day.

Vance had indicated from the first that he wished to rely wholly on prayer in Christian Science for healing, and I had called a Christian Science practitioner for him at his request. Under Christian Science treatment his condition improved visibly day by day. There was no lengthy period of recuperation as predicted. His full recovery was evident in about a week-and-a-half.

Dr. _____, a local physician, examined Vance a few days after he arrived home. The blood tests he took at that time confirmed the diagnosis of rheumatic fever. Dr. _____ advised us that Vance's "sed" rate would measure his recovery, and we were told that he would probably have to remain out of school until the next September. Dr. _____ then started to set up a schedule of office visits and monthly hospital appointments at which time the tests would be repeated. Vance asked, instead, that he be allowed to have the hospital tests again the very next week. Dr. _____ stated that the results could not possibly change that fast. However, at Vance's insistence, he agreed to authorize the tests.

The tests were given at St. Joseph's Hospital in Kokomo, Indiana, and I drove Vance there at the appointment time. When Dr. _____ called with the results, he reported that the "sed" rate had indeed changed and reached its normal level. He expressed surprise at this result and strongly recommended that if Vance did go back to college the tests be administered again in two or three weeks to be sure there was no mistake. Vance did return to school the next Monday, having missed only ten school days. The tests were given again at Hanover in about two weeks, and the results again showed a complete return to normalcy.

An incident in lighter vein, which Mrs. Patterson did not include in her affidavit, may deserve mention. As she later recounted it, the doctor who had prescribed twelve to fifteen aspirin a day asked, on the boy's next visit, "Did you take those aspirin I told you to take?"

"No."

"Why didn't you take them?"

"I didn't want to."

"What," somewhat brusquely, "would you do if you broke your leg?"

"Well," laconically, "I wouldn't take aspirin."

The letter that follows was sent to The Mother Church by a Christian Scientist from Newton, Massachusetts, Mrs. Carolyn Bloomfield. Her husband, Dr. Richard A. Bloomfield, a cardiologist who has taught for many years at Boston University and Harvard Medical School, appended to her letter a signed, handwritten note: "The events my wife has chronicled took place as described." Her account has been considerably abridged to fit into this chapter, but the selected passages adequately convey its message.

Letter from Carolyn Bloomfield of Newton, Massachusetts, in July 1982

Now that the youngest of our six children is in his first year of college, perhaps it would be appropriate to take the time to express my deepest gratitude for the well-being of our entire family which the study of Christian Science has brought.

I was a widow with two young sons at the time I found out about Christian Science; almost simultaneously, I met the man who would become my husband. He was a widower with one small son, a doctor specializing in cardiology, and an associate professor of medicine. I sent him copies of the metaphysical articles which appear in the Christian Science Monitor, with translations into the languages in which he had majored in college. I told him that I was becoming very interested in the study and living of this religion and if he felt that there might be conflicts between his profession and my growing beliefs, perhaps our friendship should not grow any deeper. Not only did he think that the translations were impressive, but felt that there could be no conflict with a religion which was based on God and was devoted to the expression of love and peace and well being. And so it has proved for these past twenty two years.

This deepening and strengthening in our understanding of

God did not come in a minute, but appeared slowly and steadily, and I persisted. . . .

I am constantly grateful for the sustained good health of our family; indeed, I don't think that the combined absence days from school for the six children could have exceeded twenty throughout all the years from nursery school to college. . . .

My first test of physical healing came when our eldest daughter was still a baby. The family was due to leave for a weekend trip when my husband returned from his work. However, I told him that I felt that our little daughter was so unwell that perhaps she and I shouldn't go. He went to look at her and told me that she needed help. He said he didn't care which I called, a practitioner or a doctor, but that I should call for help right away. Up to now, I had only called the practitioner for dispositional problems, but I had seen such solid evidences of God's presence in the working out of these difficulties that, after a moment of thought, I called for help in Christian Science. The practitioner at once assured me that this child was created by God in His image and likeness, and that in His love, as the Bible states, there is no fear. . . . In the morning my daughter's temperature had subsided somewhat. The practitioner recommended that I play some of the Christian Science hymns; this seemed strange to me, but I bundled the little girl in a blanket and propped her up on the couch in my husband's study, and we both listened while the record was playing. At the end of half an hour she was completely healed. As God's omnipresence filled my thought, all fear was dispelled, and the child responded to this sense of peace and began to express her usual joy and well-being. . . .

There are many instances of the healing truths which our children have demonstrated: a son caught and crushed his fingers in a heavy door while on a skiing trip with his father—they discussed God's presence, and His goodness, and soon the pain diminished enough to resume skiing, and the severity of the appearance disappeared in a short period of time. While at a child-care facility a son inserted a hairpin into an electrical outlet just before we picked him up. As a family, we all turned to God for peace and reassurance and soon the boy's crying ceased; by the time we removed the bandage that the nurse at the facility had applied, no evidence of what she had so vividly described could be found—and when an insurance agent came some weeks later, I could scarcely recall the incident, much less see a trace of the occurrence. . . .

[On another occasion] I had been working with the practitioner to try to help one of our boys who was having a problem in school. While attending a sports day at our daughter's school, I became aware that she was playing on a jungle gym between events, and while swinging by her knees, had fallen on her head, and was not moving. Through the assiduous work being done for our son, the sense of peace and well-being I felt could not be shaken, and I never for a moment felt anything but confidence that, no matter what the appearance might be, our daughter could never be anything but perfect. She regained her consciousness slowly, and was able to appear in her next scheduled event with zestful joy.

Years later this same girl was on the school basketball team. When I arrived at one of the games, a few minutes after it had started, she approached me with a finger that certainly looked abnormal and asked me if I would pray for her. When we arrived home after the game, I could sense that there was a feeling of unease among some of the family members, so it was decided that perhaps I should take our daughter to the hospital for an X-ray. While waiting for the development of the film, she and I began to discuss miracles, a subject under consideration in her philosophy class at school. I reminded her of what Mrs. Eddy says about miracles on page 83 of *Science and Health:* "Miracles are impossible in Science, and here Science takes issue with popular religions. The scientific manifestation of power is from the divine nature and is not supernatural, since Science is an explication of nature." When the doctor came in a few minutes later we both smiled as he said: "A miracle has happened." He went on to explain that the finger had been broken in many pieces, but that the bone was now perfectly aligned and needed only a splint to hold it in place. We thanked him and returned home in time to join the rest of the family for a weekend of skiing. After a few days of skiing and normal activity, the splint deteriorated, and that was the end of that! . . .

And I am grateful for my [own] healings over the year; the dropping away of smoking and social drinking, arthritis, sinus problems, hemorroids, unpleasant dispositional traits. . . .

My husband and children share in my gratitude for all that Christian Science has brought into our home—good health, a loving atmosphere (and that takes work and consecrated study as much as good health does!), a boundless knowledge of God's goodness, and a reliance on Him to meet all of our needs. Christian Science has made it possible to enjoy and love each other because it has enabled us to know that God enjoys and loves all of His creation, and that means us, and everyone, everywhere, in the infinite family of man.

CHAPTER 7

A Cloud of Witnesses

. . . Seeing we also are compassed about with so great a cloud of
witnesses . . .   HEBREWS 12:1

It is always possible for a determined critic to dismiss a single
spiritual healing as a case of mistaken diagnosis or spontaneous
remission. If the recovery occurs suddenly or gradually after an
individual turns to Christian Science for help, a congenital skeptic can still bring in the long arm of coincidence to knock down
any assumption that Christian Science treatment had something
to do with the healing. But when one recognizes that the few
examples chosen for inclusion in this book can be multiplied by
thousands of similar experiences during the past hundred years,
coincidence becomes a very shaky argument.

In selecting examples I have made no effort to be systematic
or to categorize them in terms of the disease or injury healed.
My overriding concern has been with the various sorts of relationship with the medical world that they illustrate. Few published testimonies go into the kind of detail found in many of
these affidavits. A number of cases described in the affidavits
have not even appeared previously as published testimonies.

This in turn points to a fact that should not be overlooked.
The tens of thousands of testimonies published in the Christian
Science periodicals over the years bear witness to only a fraction
of the healings that have actually taken place. Out of curiosity I
have often asked people who have experienced especially remarkable healings and who express great gratitude for them
verbally whether they have written them down and sent them
in for publication. The answer is far more often no than yes.
The story of Jesus and the ten lepers still has its point.

The testimonies in this chapter were chosen more or less at

random as further examples of what William James might have called "the varieties of religio-medical experience." In their various ways they provide a little more evidence of why so many people in the past century have come to regard spiritual healing as a normal and even essential element of Christian life. It is interesting to note the background of experience that has led many of the testifiers quoted in this book to become eventually public practitioners of Christian Science. Careless writers have sometimes stated erroneously that the only training required of an aspirant for this role is the two-week course of "class instruction" that most seriously committed Christian Scientists take at one time or another. An article on the Christian Science practitioner in the *Journal of Pastoral Counseling* puts the matter more realistically:

The training for this task begins with the individual's first commitment to the study of Christian Science. Basically this is a self-conducted study, centering on the Bible and the Christian Science textbook *Science and Health with Key to the Scriptures* by Mary Baker Eddy. From the outset it imposes a strict discipline on the serious student. The Word was made flesh, he is emphatically reminded; the abstract must become concrete, understanding be tested in healing, ontological concepts be related to life situations, if he is to make any real progress.

At some point he must complete a short course of intensive instruction from an authorized teacher of Christian Science, but the chief and continuing emphasis is on his daily practice of a discipline which includes the demand for practical results as well as for prayer, study, application, and spiritual growth. There is no resting satisfied with the advancement made at any given point, since nothing less than the New Testament record of instantaneous healing is the standard of achievement held before him.[1]

The intensive two-week course consists of three or four hours of classroom instruction daily, plus a heavy reading and writing assignment. Together with other preparation for the next day's lesson, this can mean from five to eight additional hours' study each day. The emphasis is on learning how to study as well as how to practice, and, brief as the experience is, observation shows that it often turns an eager but untried enthusiast into a committed, hard-working student and healer for the rest of his or her life. Yearly association meetings of teacher and students serve as one-day refresher courses, and through the years there is often a close, one-to-one relation of counsel and help between teacher and student. But the greatest lessons, most practitioners would agree, are learned in the laboratory of living and the silent sanctuary of prayer.

Mention should also be made of the training of Christian Science nurses. The first three affidavits that follow refer to Christian Science nursing facilities, especially two sanatoriums in Boston and San Francisco now known respectively as the Chestnut Hill Benevolent Association and the Arden Wood Benevolent Association. At these two institutions and two others in Princeton, New Jersey, and London, England, three-year training courses are held for Christian Science nurses under the sponsorship of The Mother Church. The training is nonmedical but covers such areas as basic nursing arts (bandaging, bathing, bed making, and so forth), care for the elderly, cooking for invalids, and above all maintaining an atmosphere that supports the patient's own spiritual endeavors.

Affidavit of Dorothy D. Wilson of Amherst, New Hampshire, in May 1982

I was raised as a Christian Scientist and have been a member of the Church of Christ, Scientist, for the last thirty-four years. I've experienced and witnessed many healings through that time, but two related experiences stand out in my memory.

In 1953, when my children were young, I developed a large uterine tumor that caused increasing pressure and pain over a period of nine months. We were living in Grosse Pointe City, Michigan, at that time, and I was a member of the Christian Science congregation which was just then starting up in Grosse Pointe. I had the help of two Christian Science practitioners at different periods during the nine months of this experience, and was much sustained by their prayer and love.

My husband, who was not a Christian Scientist, expressed a great deal of alarm at my condition. So did several of my neighbors, including a radiologist, Dr. _____, of _____ Road in Grosse Point City. Dr. _____ asked to be allowed to arrange for X-rays, and I consented because of my husband's concern. I went to Harper Hospital to have the X-rays taken in October 1954. These revealed a large tumor. The specialist who examined them stated that I should have it surgically removed within 48 hours.

At this point I told my husband that I wished to go to a sanatorium for Christian Scientists. He agreed to this, and I made arrangements for a trip to the Chestnut Hill Benevolent Association in Chestnut Hill, Massachusetts. On the way to the airport I was in such severe pain that I was unable even to sit up in the car. After arriving at my destination, I called a local Christian Science practitioner who agreed to help through prayer.

I remained in the sanatorium for the next two weeks. I spent this time in prayer and study and often walked outside on the grounds singing hymns. The pain lessened and then faded entirely. The physical evidence of the tumor gradually disappeared. I left a changed person, both physically and mentally, and resumed all my normal activities.

Three years later, in 1957, the problem recurred. We were then living in New Canaan, Connecticut. Actually, there was no pain at all this time. I learned of the condition after experiencing what seemed to be several of the symptoms of pregnancy. In fact, I went to a leading gynecologist in _____, Dr. _____, who examined me and informed me that I was definitely pregnant. I visited the doctor for regular check-ups over the next six months. The rabbit tests proved negative, but he continued to insist nevertheless that I was pregnant. When I asked if there was any possibility that the symptoms might stem from a tumor, he said no and explained that the growth rate of a tumor was quite distinct from that of a fetus. In the sixth month I asked the doctor to take an X-ray. He did so, and on seeing the results told me that I was not pregnant after all but had a very large and very serious tumor. That was a Friday, and he stated that I should have an operation the following Monday. I told him, however, that I preferred to rely on prayer in Christian Science for healing.

Our family had been planning a trip to an island in Maine where we owned a house. I told my husband that I wanted to go early by myself to be alone with God. I spent the next week praying, walking the beaches, and studying the Bible and the Christian Science textbook. This was in August 1957. I felt less fear about the condition, really, than disappointment over the fact that I wasn't to have a third child. During that week in

Maine, however, I gained a clear sense of God's ever-present love. I'd always felt God to be the focal point of my life, but now sought to acknowledge more deeply that divine Love is truly in control of every facet of existence. And by the time the family joined me a week or so after I had arrived, I knew I had had my healing—permanently. The tumor diminished until all evidence of it was gone. My weight returned to normal within another week, and I put aside the maternity clothes I had been wearing.

That was 25 years ago now. There has never been a recurrence. I never returned to be examined by the physician who had diagnosed the tumor—nor did he even send me a bill for those six months of visits. I've led a very vigorous life since that time and have continued to turn to God as my only physician.

Affidavit of Alice Thompson of Seattle, Washington, in May 1982

On April 26, 1970, I fell while dancing. I was carried to the house of some friends, Mr. and Mrs. Marion Smidowski in Seattle, and when I arrived, called a Christian Science practitioner for help through prayer. After five days I decided to have an X-ray, as I still could not walk. On May 1, Mr. and Mrs. Smidowski, who are not Christian Scientists, took me to their physician, Dr. A ____, whose office is now at _____ Road. After taking X-rays, he told my friends to take me right over to the emergency entrance of _____ Hospital in _____, a suburb of Seattle, to see a specialist.

At the hospital I was examined by Dr. B ____, who took further X-rays and informed me that my hip was badly broken— an incomplete fracture of the femoral neck on the right side. He asked me, "Aren't you in excruciating pain?" I told him that I was having treatment through prayer from a Christian Science practitioner and had felt almost no pain since the time of the accident. Dr. B ____ then stated that I would need to have a pin surgically placed in the hip. I explained, however, that as a Christian Scientist I had long relied on prayer for healing. I wanted to pray further and listen for God's answer, and told the doctor I would have to go home and make my own decision. I left the hospital after signing a release.

The next day Dr. B ____'s secretary called, stating that the doctor had requested her to call me to ask again if I would consent to the surgery he had recommended. The doctor himself then took the phone and explained again the seriousness of the fracture. I thanked him for his kind concern but indicated that I had decided to rely wholly on prayer in Christian Science for the healing. He asked if I would come for a further examination in a few more weeks, and I agreed.

That day I traveled to the New Haven sanatorium, now called Sunrise House/Newhaven, a care facility for Christian Scientists in Puyallup, Washington. While there, I remained in contact with the Christian Science practitioner whom I had asked for help through prayer. I was at New Haven for two weeks. From the morning after I arrived I was active and dressed each day and even played the organ, which required me to stretch my right leg to reach the pedals. For the first few days I used a wheelchair to move about. After a week or so I was able to walk without support or assistance. I still had a slight limp when I left the facility in mid-May, but this cleared up completely in a little over a month. I resumed most of my normal daily activities from the time I left the sanatorium.

I went back to see Dr. B ____ at his office . . . , as he had requested, on June 16, 1970. After taking X-rays, Dr. B ____ put his arm around my shoulders and told me that my hip was even stronger than it would have been if he had put a pin in it. In a letter he wrote for me to take to work, he indicated that the normal recuperation period for a fracture of this nature was four months.

I was fifty-nine years old at the time of this healing. Since then I have continued to lead a vigorous life—dancing three or four times a week and even teaching a folk dancing class. The healing has been permanent, and I have had complete freedom of movement in all my many activities.

Affidavit of Betty Fiedler of Wichita, Kansas, in November 1982

I was still newly interested in Christian Science when a challenging physical disease manifested itself and resulted in complications, including heart trouble and loss of weight. This was in 1961. I was then living in Denver, Colorado. My condition deteriorated over the next months; my eyes and my appearance altered alarmingly. My family and close friends urged me to consult a physician, and I did.

The first physician to whom I went for examination was Dr. A____ in Denver. He referred me to two specialists, Dr. B____ and Dr. C____, also then practicing in Denver. I underwent an extensive examination that included blood and metabolism tests. Dr. C ____, a surgeon, informed me that I had a toxic hyperthyroid condition requiring immediate surgery for the removal of the thyroid gland. He stated that my metabolism rate was four times normal and that even after the operation I would need continuing drug treatment. The doctor's office was near a hospital, and he advised me to go there immediately and have myself admitted as his patient. He explained that I would need to be placed under heavy sedation for several days before the operation.

I did not enter the hospital. Dr. C____ telephoned me several days later to urge me to enter this or another hospital of my choice as soon as possible, telling me flatly that the condition would be terminal unless I had the recommended operation. At this point, however, I understood enough from reading the textbooks of Christian Science—the King James Bible and *Science and Health* by Mrs. Eddy—to know that I could be healed through spiritual regeneration and growth. Thus I asked a Christian Science practitioner for help through prayer and arranged to travel to the Christian Science Benevolent Association in San Francisco, where I could devote myself to gaining a deeper understanding of God and my relationship to Him.

I remained at the Benevolent Association for approximately three weeks. My days were spent almost wholly in prayer. By the end of my stay, my consciousness was so illumined I knew I was healed, even though at the time there was no change in my physical appearance. The first outward sign of the healing came in church one Sunday, when I turned to the window and was able to look into the sunlight without difficulty for the first time since the problem developed. As I held fast to the new spiritual view of myself I had gained, my body soon manifested normalcy. Within a month of leaving the sanatorium, all symptoms of the thyroid condition had departed and I was completely healed.

It has now been twenty years since this healing. There has

been no recurrence whatsoever. Soon after the healing I joined a branch church of Christ, Scientist. I have continued to rely on prayer in Christian Science for healing in all the years since.

Testimony of Friedrich Roselius, Lohhof, Federal Republic of Germany, in the Christian Science Sentinel, July 14, 1980

[Original in German]

From earliest childhood I had suffered from the symptoms of a stubborn case of eczema. Over the years the disease spread with increasing severity to various parts of my body. Each day it became more unbearable. In school, and later in my profession, this condition seemed an insurmountable obstacle. Twenty-five years of medical treatment had failed to bring the slightest improvement. I had been told that in my case the eczema was hereditary, which seemed to make it especially defiant of cure. And so the pattern continued, and I simply put up with it.

Finally, through an acquaintance of my mother's, I learned of Christian Science. It was a landmark occasion! As I read *Science and Health*, which derives its authority from the Bible, I began to glimpse the reality of God, including divine Mind's absolute control. It was also evident that God, as immortal Life, is not the creator of sickness, and this precludes sickness as a possibility. In *Science and Health* Mrs. Eddy explains (p. 390), "It is our ignorance of God, the divine Principle, which produces apparent discord, and the right understanding of Him restores harmony."

With joy I noticed that after I had begun regular study of the Bible Lesson in the *Christian Science Quarterly*, my general state of health took a substantial turn for the better. A chronic thyroid ailment disappeared, and there was no longer susceptibility to frequent colds. When I realized that I could work successfully with the truths of Christian Science and apply them practically, I decided to become a member of The Mother Church and of a branch of Church of Christ, Scientist.

As I grew spiritually, my scientific relationship to God became more certain to me. Nevertheless, as strange as it might sound, despite the healings I had accomplished through Science, it had not yet occurred to me that I could be freed from the eczema. One day, however, when the condition became more aggravated, I decided to discuss it with a Christian Science practitioner. He assured me that disease is a mortal belief that has never belonged to the man of God's creating. In my real being as God's idea, the image of Spirit, I was subject solely to the irrefutable law of perfection and wholeness. My only true inheritance was a rich abundance of divine good. This conversation strengthened my conviction that all types of discord had been healed through Christian Science, and that once an error has been destroyed by infinite Truth, it can never return.

Immediately after our talk, there was noticeable improvement in my condition. Four days later there wasn't a trace of the eczema to be found. The skin on my hands, feet, and other parts of my body was renewed, and I now had completely smooth and healthy fingernails. A gratitude unlike any I'd known welled within me. This healing took place some years ago, and there has been no recurrence of the eczema. Christian Science has shown me that spiritual healing involves a purification of consciousness, releasing one from the collective belief that sickness is an inevitable necessity against which man is helpless. Wherever God is, man is never helpless, and God is everywhere.

In a confirmatory letter of September 26, 1982, the testifier's mother, Mrs. Claire Roselius, listed seventeen of the doctors who had treated her son over a twenty-two-year period. They are listed below for the story they suggest by their sheer multiplicity:

Dr. Sommerfeld	Prakt. Arzt	Kassel	zu versheid
Dr. Leibich	Internist	Tegernsee	1940/41
Dr. Leibich	Internist	Tegernsee	1940/41
Dr. Held	Internist	Miesbach	1940/41
Dr. Risch	Internist	Miesbach	1940/41
Dr. Froberg	Internist	Tegernsee	1940/41
Dr. Vogel	Prakt. Arzt	Tegernsee	1940/41
Dr. Raba	Prakt. Arzt	Obermenzing	1944/49
Dr. Peters	Dermatologe	Kassel	1955
Dr. Schwarz	Prakt. Arzt	Kassel	1955
Dr. Herzberger	Prakt. Arzt	Kassel	1955
Dr. Ide	Prakt. Arzt	Kassel	1955
Dr. Schöne	Internist	Obermenzing	1956
Dr. Frank		München	1956
Dr. Rupp	Obermenzing/Nymphenburg		1956
Prof. Dr. Bermann	Internist	München	
Dr. Schmitt	Prakt. Arzt	Oberminzing	
Dr. Engelberg	Prakt. Arzt	Stockdorf	1957-61

The letter of Frau Roselius makes an interesting allusion to the placebo effect that some of these doctors' treatments had for a time without ever effecting a permanent healing. Her explanation (in translation) follows: "Each of these doctors applied his own methods in accordance with his best experiences, and the new hope that we took with us each time would sometimes cause the start of a new treatment to seem effective at first. But a healing never came about."

Affidavit of Lois Drake of North Royalton, Ohio, in September 1982

Christian Science first came into my life many years ago when I was employed by a man who was a Scientist. I had been opposed to what I thought Christian Science was, but he and his family expressed so much love and joy that I began to get a different opinion of it. At times I read the textbook, *Science and Health with Key to the Scriptures*, by Mary Baker Eddy. I attended church services occasionally and went to Christian Science lectures, but I was never a really devoted student.

In 1947, a few months after my marriage, I became seriously ill. We were living in Strongsville, Ohio. On the recommendation of our family physician, Dr. _____ of Strongsville, I went to the _____ Hospital in _____ for tests and X-rays. The diagnosis was tuberculosis of the spine.

I was told by the physicians at the hospital that I would have to go into a sanatorium where I would be placed in a body cast for a year and a half while the spine healed. I asked to be released from the hospital so that I might make a decision. After three days of soul-searching I decided that I would turn wholly to God for the healing and called a Christian Science practitioner for treatment through prayer.

My family opposed my decision and tried to convince me to have medical treatment. Dr. _____, who was a lifelong friend, urged the family to have me taken to specialists for further tests. In view of the family fears, I went to the _____ Clinic (which is now located at _____ Avenue in _____) where I was given extensive examination. This included tests of fluid from an abscess on my body, which proved positive. The results all confirmed the earlier diagnosis, and the prognosis given was even worse than before: three years in a body cast. I was told that my condition would deteriorate rapidly without this course of treatment. The doctors at the clinic informed me that I was also suffering from pernicious anemia.

In spite of these findings I chose to have continued prayerful help in Christian Science. I did not wear a body cast, and at no time did I take medication for the condition. My fear began to lessen somewhat when I didn't get worse, as had been predicted. I was not employed during this time but was able to move about the house as I pleased and take care of myself.

I was in touch with the Christian Science practitioner daily and devoted much time to study of the Bible and Christian Science literature. The Christian Science Hymnal was a great comfort to me, as were these words from the Christian Science textbook, page 264: "We must look where we would walk, and we must act as possessing all power from Him in whom we have our being." This verse from 2 Timothy (1:7) was also particularly helpful: "For God hath not given us the spirit of fear; but of power, and of love, and of a sound mind."

Within three months' time I returned to work and resumed a normal active life, fully healed. Later I joined the Church of Christ, Scientist. The healing has been permanent, and its completeness was demonstrated a year later when my first child was born. Her birth was normal, free of complications. There has been no recurrence of the condition whatever; I have not even experienced a backache in all the years since then!

Testimonial by Bettie B. Thompson of Washington, D.C., published in The Christian Science Journal, May 1979

One time when my husband and I were having a business problem, a friend urged us to talk with a Christian Science practitioner. Our friend had sent us several religious articles from *The Christian Science Monitor*. To satisfy him, we made an appointment with a practitioner.

I had read some Christian Science literature that used the word "treatment," and during the visit I wondered aloud what that meant. The practitioner asked if I wanted treatment, and after gaining my consent, she prayed for me on the spot. I was asked to read the Lord's Prayer, with its spiritual interpretation given by Mary Baker Eddy in *Science and Health* (pp. 16, 17). My husband was requested to read this passage from the Bible (Isa. 41:10): "Fear thou not; for I am with thee: be not dismayed; for I am thy God: I will strengthen thee; yea, I will help thee; yea, I will uphold thee with the right hand of my righteousness. '' This remarkable woman, a descendant of African slaves, prayed silently, and our visit was over in less than an hour.

A few days later I realized that a lump in my breast, for which I had received unsuccessful medical treatment, had disappeared.

This healing pricked our curiosity. I began going to the railroad and bus stations to get free Christian Science literature out of the distribution boxes. Then at home I'd read them from cover to cover. These magazines opened up a whole new world for me.

At this time, nine years ago, my husband was suffering from glaucoma. He could hardly see objects held right in front of his face. The condition frightened and depressed us. Periodically we went to a doctor, who checked the eye condition and gave him medicine for it. My husband was told that if the medication was discontinued he would go blind in six months.

Meanwhile, we talked to a practitioner about our interest in Christian Science and the problem confronting us. She told us to continue study of the Bible and *Science and Health* to find out more about ourselves and about God, and she declared, "God loves you." This was wonderful to hear that divine Love is always protecting us. We were beginning to understand man's true nature as God's perfect reflection.

We had to make a decision. Did my husband want to stay in that condition, since there was no medical cure for the glaucoma? Or would we try Christian Science? We decided to rely on Christian Science for healing. My husband abandoned the medicine and had help from a practitioner. Gradually his sight improved. This was over a period of three months. One day we went to a Christian Science lecture. During the lecture his vision cleared totally. He was free from the former pain and pressure—completely healed.

The following Sunday, my husband recommended we attend the Church of Christ, Scientist, a request that surprised me since we were both actively involved in another denomination. We were inspired by the music and, above all, the substantial readings from the Bible and *Science and Health*.

After our two startling healings, we decided we wouldn't receive just the "loaves and fishes" without giving something in return. We decided right then that we would learn more about Christian Science and help share it with others. We felt if Mrs. Eddy could devote her lifetime to helping mankind, then we would share the little we knew of divine Science with our fellowmen.

We have had a complete spiritual renewal. We are grateful that Christian Science has blessed us and brought us much comfort.

Affidavit of Mr. Thompson in December 1982

Mr. Dolphin G. Thompson, being first duly sworn, deposes and says:

That the healing of glaucoma related in my wife's testimonial published in the May 1979 issue of *The Christian Science Journal* took place as described. The glaucoma was first diagnosed in 1965 by Dr. A____, an ophthalmologist practicing in Washington, D.C. He prescribed eye medication and the use of glasses. I obtained the glasses and took the medication regularly over the next two years. It was Dr. A____ who informed me that I would go blind from the condition if the medication were discontinued.

In 1967 I consulted a second specialist, Dr. B____, chief of ophthalmology at the _____ University Hospital. He confirmed the diagnosis of glaucoma but prescribed different medication. At the time, he indicated that I would need to continue using this medication indefinitely. I did so for the next year until turning wholly to Christian Science. During this period I visited Dr. B____ periodically for examination, and the condition of the eyes remained substantially unchanged.

The healing took place in 1968 and has been permanent. Since then my vision has been normal. I see and read clearly without glasses today, a fact attested by the vision tests I have taken for renewal of my driver's license.

Epilepsy is held to be a somewhat mysterious disease whose violence sometimes abates in time, for unknown reasons—possibly as a result of that equally mysterious force known in medical literature as *vis medicatrix naturae*. The two following accounts, representative of many others in Christian Science literature, point to a more spiritual and less recognized possibility.

Certified statement of Freni Wadia of London, England, in December 1982

When I was about fifteen and living in Bangalore, India, I began to have attacks of epilepsy which were so severe that I used to be bedridden from five days to a week. After some years of trying different doctors and different systems of medicine, and spending much money, my parents took me to the

Vellore Hospital in Madras State, a missionary hospital re-
nowned as one of the best teaching hospitals, where I was
treated by the foremost doctors and neurologists in the country.
After extensive tests involving X-rays of the brain and spinal
column and much else, I was put on drugs and tranquilizers.
Being constantly on drugs I went through life only half awake.
I had no choice but to take the soporific drugs which prevented
me from using my faculties fully, for the fear of a sudden attack
hung over me like a sword.

Upon finishing school I was unable to take up the career of
my choice, as epilepsy disqualified me from being a teacher of
young children. I therefore decided to become a doctor. I attended Mysore University in Bangalore for four years but failed
to get my pre-medical degree. I took up an office job to earn
my living but was never happy. I visited places of worship of
other faiths that purported to heal and comfort, only to return
more depressed and dejected.

In 1953 one of my sisters returned from a visit to Bombay
and brought with her *Science and Health with Key to the Scriptures*
by Mary Baker Eddy, the Christian Science textbook. I began to
read it eagerly but was bitterly disappointed because at that
time it said nothing to me. Over the years I read the book off
and on, wondering all the time what message it held within its
pages, but I had to go through deeper trials before my heart
was prepared to receive what the book had to say to me. From
time to time I tried giving up the drugs but always the attacks
returned and I became increasingly aware of the burden I was
becoming to my family, so that I always returned to the drug
regime.

In 1961 I had the opportunity of going to England. All my
family agreed that a change of scene might do me good and
even if it did not I could consult the best neurologists in that
country. I stayed in Putney near London and consulted a local
doctor, Dr. _____. He referred me to the _____ Hospital where
again I underwent tests, but I was quite disillusioned because
the same drugs were prescribed.

I became increasingly depressed over the following two years
but remained in London. In mid 1963 I again took up *Science
and Health* in order to gain a sense of peace and freedom from
the fear of attacks but brought to it a new receptivity. By 1964 I

felt ready to rely upon Christian Science on the strength of what I had gained from reading *Science and Health,* but I thought it fair to tell my family what I was proposing to do because I was aware of the responsibility that they felt for me. I then gave up all drugs and turned wholly to the understanding that I was gaining of God. In fact I gained not only the peace I sought, but found I was completely healed, and I have never since suffered from an attack.

What came to me during that year of reading *Science and Health* was an awareness of my relationship to God in which I was able to find my true spiritual selfhood, and I drew on these spiritual resources to face up to and overcome my deepest fears and worries. I also experienced a profound transformation of character and thought.

My desire to be a teacher was fulfilled for I was able to go out of London on a teaching job and live on my own for the first time in the forty years of my life. For this purpose I had to pass the usual rigorous medical tests under a doctor appointed by the Education Authority. This healing took place solely through my own reading of *Science and Health.*

In the years since, I have felt a profound gratitude that in Christian Science I was able to find my way to the healing Christ, as available and active today as it was two thousand years ago in the life of our Lord.

And I make this solemn declaration conscientiously believing the same to be true and by virtue of the provisions of the Statutory Declarations Act 1835.

Affidavit of Harold F. Green of West Chester, Pennsylvania, in February 1983

In the fall of 1970 an advertising representative from a local branch Church of Christ, Scientist, called on me to place an ad in *The Christian Science Monitor.* I did advertise my business for several months. At Christmas time, a member of the branch church called on me to buy a TV set. The model she was interested in had to be ordered.

Previous to this visit I had been ill with recurring attacks of epilepsy (grand mal). The attacks had begun about two years earlier. The condition was originally diagnosed at _____ Hospital in _____, Pennsylvania, where I was taken during the first attack. Our family physician, Dr. A_____ of _____, referred me to a neurologist in the area, Dr. B ____, whom I visited regularly until my decision to turn to Christian Science.

Dr. B____ prescribed increasingly strong drug dosages in an effort to control the symptoms. In spite of the drugs, however, the attacks continued. In early 1971 Dr. B____ informed me that he suspected the cause of the problem might be a brain tumor, and I entered _____ Hospital again for two weeks of tests by a team of specialists. These tests were extremely arduous, and during those two weeks I lost 25 pounds. The tests were negative for brain tumor, but Dr. B ____ informed me that there was no cure for the epileptic condition and that I would need to remain on a drug regimen indefinitely to control the attacks.

I returned to my business in a very depressed state. Not long thereafter the Christian Scientist who had ordered the TV came to the store to pick it up. The drastic change in my physical condition was evident. She asked what had happened. I told her, then asked if Christian Science could help. She began to explain that healing in Christian Science comes through prayer, spiritual understanding, gaining a deeper sense of man's relationship to God.

We talked these things over at length in the next few weeks. At my request she gave me Christian Science periodicals to read and explained the study of the Bible lesson sermons in the *Christian Science Quarterly*. She also invited me to a Christian Science church service, an invitation I warmly accepted. I found that new contentedness came to me. I was learning to live one day at a time and to let God work out His purpose for me.

Initially I felt uneasy about abandoning the pills. At no time was I pressured to do so by the Christian Scientist, though she explained to me the wholly spiritual basis of healing in Christian Science. I continued to take the drugs prescribed for several months after starting to study Christian Science seriously. At one point I stopped taking them for a week, had another attack, and went back to them. But increasingly I gained the conviction that I could turn to God for healing. Also, the side effects of the drugs were becoming disturbing. Dr. B____ said there was no way to avert these effects and in fact advised stronger medication for the continuing epileptic symptoms. I felt there must be a better way. Thus, when the prescriptions I was taking ran out, I did not have them refilled but asked the Christian Scientist with whom I had been speaking for help through prayer.

I continued to have help in Christian Science over the next months. Although I was taking no medication, the attacks soon became fewer and further apart. Within less than a year of turning to Christian Science, the attacks had ceased altogether. This was in 1972, and the healing has been permanent. I regained my health and weight and again became enthusiastic about life. I am in excellent health and am an active member of The Mother Church and a branch church.

Declaration of Gunilla Eleonora Berglund of Stockholm,
Sweden, in January 1983

On July 9, 1974, I was busy painting the outside of our shop on Ranhammarsvägen in Bromma, Stockholm. I fell off a ladder and injured one knee severely. I was unable to get up, but I turned immediately to God in prayer. My husband, who is not a Christian Scientist, helped me so that I could sit, and implored me to get the leg X-rayed. He drove me to St. Erik's Hospital on Flemminggatan in Stockholm. I was examined and X-rayed in the surgery ward. After examining the X-rays, Dr. Torbjörn Ekström stated that the knee showed a compression fracture, i.e., the bone structure was jammed together in the knee. (See the physician's statement and the X-ray photographs.) The doctor explained that I must be operated on and that I must remain at the hospital until the operation the following day. However, since I had previously experienced healings through Christian Science, I chose to depend solely on prayer in Christian Science to heal the injured knee. The first result of this prayer was that the pain disappeared in a couple of hours.

I told the physician that I wanted to depend solely on prayer in Christian Science. After several attempts to persuade me to have the operation, the doctor asked me to stay at least overnight at the hospital. Since no treatment would be administered, I agreed to this. The next day I went home in an ambulance. The doctor pointed out for me that I was doing this at my own risk. He advised me to lie still for eight weeks and not put any weight whatsoever on the knee.

As soon as I arrived home I telephoned a Christian Science practitioner and asked for help through prayer. There was marked improvement with each day, and after five days I was on my feet again. After one week I went back to the hospital for a check-up. The doctor who examined me said that the knee was fine. At that point she had not seen the original X-rays. When she had, she came back and said that I could absolutely not be well, and that I must lie down immediately. In her opinion there was no way the knee could have been healed in that short time. At that point I walked back and forth in the room to prove that everything was fine. Then she called Dr. Torbjörn Ekström and several other physicians, and I had to show them that the knee supported the weight of my body.

Several days later I left for a short vacation that had been planned for a long time, during which I did a great deal of hiking. Afterward I continued working in our shop, which meant a working day of 11–13 hours where I was standing or walking most of the time.

Except for the first few hours after the fall, I felt no pain. There was no cast or bandage. Neither was there any medication. My knee is completely normal again and functions perfectly. The quick healing came solely through prayer in Christian Science.

The above healing helped me several years later in connection with a similar incident. Saturday, August 11, 1979, I slipped while going out of the house at our country place. I slid down into a hole and injured my right ankle seriously. Once again I turned immediately to God in prayer. I managed to come into the house where I lay down on a bed. My husband again pleaded with me to get the foot X-rayed. He drove me to St. Erik's Hospital in Stockholm, where my foot was X-rayed in the emergency ward. The surgeon on duty, A. Odebäck, said that the X-ray showed a "fracture of the fibula at the height of the syndesmos" and that the foot must be put in a cast.

However, the healing of the earlier broken bone through Christianly scientific prayer strengthened me in my decision, even in this case, to depend entirely upon prayer without any medical treatment. I told Dr. Odebäck of my decision. She said that I could absolutely not stand on my foot for a long time. I took out the certificate from Dr. Torbjörn Ekström from 1974 which I had taken with me when I had left for the hospital.

After reading it, Dr. Odebäck accepted my decision. She wrote out a hospital injury certificate referring the case to "Christian Science" and stating that the ankle was fractured and that I would not accept the normal treatment of putting it in a cast. I gratefully acknowledged her concern that was so clearly expressed in her desire to help me.

My husband then drove me home. During this entire time and the following days I turned continually to God in prayer as I have learned in Christian Science. On Sunday, August 12, I stayed home. During the following days my condition worsened at first. My foot had swollen so much that I couldn't wear normal shoes. Three toes were black, and my foot was discolored. I continued praying to God. I was up and walked on both feet during this entire time. Thursday, August 16, was an especially arduous day for me, since I had to be on my feet 13–14 hours in our shop. But on that day there was an obvious improvement. The swelling went down and the foot began to regain its natural color. I continued to thank God in my prayers for His wonderful care for me. On Saturday, August 18, one week after the accident, the foot had regained its normal form and color. I could put on my rubber boots and wash our car. On Saturday, August 18, my recovery was complete. At the time of writing, three years have passed since this healing occurred, and my foot has been fine since then. I didn't return to the hospital for a check-up, because I felt that I was completely healed.

This healing came about solely through my prayers to God as I have learned to pray in Christian Science.

Mrs. Berglund's account is accompanied by a certificate signed by Dr. Torbjörn Ekström on September 18, 1974, presented here in rough translation.

Declaration of Dr. Torbjörn Ekström, September 18, 1974

Mrs. Berglund applied on July 9, 1974, after falling from a ladder. At the examination it was found that her right knee was warm and swollen. X-rays of the knee showed a so-called compression fracture, i.e., a pressing together of the bone structure in the knee. This fracture affected the top part of the shinbone, the part that is part of the knee joint. The pressing together of the knee was measured on the outside to be one centimeter [0.39 inches]. The usual treatment for this is not to put any weight on the leg, i.e., that one in no way supports oneself on the leg for a time period of about eight weeks. However, the patient did not follow this prescription but was already walking on the leg after five days, and she is now, September 17, as far as one can see, totally restored with perfect function of the knee.

A brief postscript by Dr. Ekström on October 30, 1974, added the following note: "Mrs. Berglund had informed us at her very first visit that she belonged to Christian Science and intended to seek help there in order to heal her injured knee." It is very rare for a physician or surgeon to be willing to acknowledge a Christian Science cure *in writing*, although many do so verbally at the time of the healing.

Affidavit of Helen P. Sousa, then of Lexington, Massachusetts, in May 1982

In May 1954 I went for a routine eye examination to Dr. A____, an ophthalmologist at _____ Avenue in Somerville, Massachusetts. Dr. A____, to whom I had been going for examinations for two or three years, discovered what he said was a possible malignancy in the left eye. He sent me to an ophthalmological surgeon, Dr. B____, whose office was at _____ Street in Boston. After further examination, Dr. B____ diagnosed the condition as a sarcoma resting on the optic nerve at the rear of the left eye. After bringing another physician in for consultation, he told me that I must enter the hospital as soon as possible for the removal of at least the left eye and possibly of both.

I entered the Massachusetts Eye and Ear Infirmary in Boston in early June. After extensive examination, the diagnosis was confirmed by the Chief of Ophthalmology there, Dr. C____, and a team of physicians in surgical conference. Then, since I had to make arrangements to leave my job, I left the hospital temporarily, expecting to return for surgery in a few days.

A young man who worked with me was a Christian Scientist. I did not know much about the religion, but when he heard about my situation, he called me and recommended that I see a

Christian Science practitioner. I did visit the practitioner. I think the first thing that impressed me was that she didn't want to talk about my condition. Rather, she wanted to talk about the nature of Deity, what God is, and what that meant to me as His child.

I asked for Christian Science treatment through prayer and in several days began to be a bit encouraged. I went back to Dr. A___ and asked him to examine me again. He told me the condition couldn't possibly have changed, but finally agreed to re-examine the eye. And when he did he found no change. Of course this was very bad news, and I lost hope. I called the Christian Science practitioner to thank her for her help and to tell her that I felt I had no choice but to go in to the hospital for surgery. She assured me that prayer was effective and that I could rest in God no matter where I was or what condition I was in.

I entered the Eye and Ear Infirmary for the operation as scheduled. However, in the pre-surgical examination, Dr. C___ and the other physicians did discover a change in my condition. There was a further examination at another surgical conference, in which one of the physicians on the team likened the change to entering a familiar house and finding a totally new backyard. The doctors informed me that immediate surgery was no longer necessary, but suggested that I come in at least weekly for observation and examination. I got myself dismissed from the hospital as soon as I could, called the practitioner again, and told her I was going to rely on Christian Science for healing.

We prayed together for several months. At this time I was beginning to experience very disturbing symptoms—severe pain, blackouts, nausea, loss of sight, and loss of weight. I became very fearful. For the first month or so I did return periodically to Dr. B___ for examination, though not for medication. The physical symptoms were worsening. Somewhere around mid-summer I realized that I was still trying to hold on to material as well as spiritual means, so I decided to take a firm stand with Christian Science. When I told Dr. B___ that I would not be returning for further examination, he expressed great concern and upbraided me sternly. He asked at one point, "Do you think I want to see you walk away and die?" But I felt that I needed to place my full trust in God. I kept praying with the Christian Science practitioner through the summer. By September, all the symptoms of the sarcoma just dropped away. I was completely healed, and my health has been excellent ever since.

I should mention that the physicians at the hospital, in attempting to explain the change in the eye, suggested that the condition might have been a birthmark to begin with. But Dr. A____ stated flatly that there had been no such mark evident prior to May 1954 and that he could not possibly have missed such a mark in the previous eye examinations he had given me. The optometrist whom I had consulted for many years while growing up, Dr. D____ of Cambridge, also affirmed that there had been no birthmark.

Following her healing, Miss Sousa served for many years as an executive in the treasurer's office of The Mother Church before her death in 1984 from a cause completely unrelated to the foregoing problem. In telling her office colleagues of that experience, she would sometimes contrast a little wryly the astronomical sum she paid the medical specialists with the almost ridiculously modest fee of the Christian Science practitioner through whose prayer the healing came.

People often suppose that Christian Science healing is a matter of willpower. Like all true Christian healing, it actually involves (in New Testament terms) the surrender of one's own will to God's. But as the next account indicates, this very surrender can open the way for the moral courage, faith, persistence, and heroism necessary during a protracted period of healing. These values can be quite as important in a spiritual healing as in a medical situation—or in the partial involvement with medicine this experience included.

Statutory declaration of Fiona Pope of Glasgow, Scotland, in January 1983

During the war in 1944 I was widowed, hours after being married. My parents had their home completely destroyed, and I suffered a nervous breakdown which affected my sight.

In 1946 for health reasons I went on a trip overseas and on my return I first learned of Christian Science through a friend and my first glimpse followed of the meaning of the Bible promise that "all things are possible to God."

In September 1947 I contracted polio during a local epidemic. My parents called the doctor, but they also told the Christian Scientist friend of my condition. I was taken to the local hospital in Johnstone, Renfrewshire and put in isolation, almost wholly paralysed. I was unable to swallow or speak, my kidneys were almost out of action, and I found it very difficult to breathe. For one month I remained in isolation, lying on my back with arms immobilised, only able to gaze at the ceiling and in acute distress. Throughout this time my slight acquaintance with Christian Science was a great comfort to me. I dwelt on favourite verses of the Bible, and I remembered a sentence that my friend had brought to my attention from the Christian Science textbook *Science and Health:* "Be firm in your understanding that the divine Mind governs," which was all I knew of the sentence. My breathing was so laboured that I was given to understand that if the only iron lung in the hospital had not been in use by a boy in the nextdoor bed I would have been on it. Yet the strong conviction grew that my new-found faith was healing me. Although I do not know whether, or what kind of, medical treatment was being given during this time, my parents were in touch with a Christian Science practitioner.

After a month I was moved to Philipshill Hospital where my whole body was put in plaster. The sister [nurse, in the U.S.A.] who was in charge of the ward told me without, I am sure, any intention to be unkind, that I might never walk again, but that if I was to be capable of any movement it would not be until the following spring. By now I was receiving help from a practitioner, which continued throughout my recovery, and was not receiving any medical treatment. Within a few days of arriving at the new hospital and with the assistance of two nurses, I walked a few steps, to the extent that the plaster permitted. Within a few days after that I was visited by a specialist and asked to be allowed to go home. I was sent home in a taxi with my arms stretched out in front still encased in plaster. I consciously accepted as little limitation as possible, tidied my bedroom as far as I was able, and devised a means of using the sewing machine. Step by step my strength returned. I did not submit to any muscular therapy or other outpatient treatment.

The plaster was for the purposes of support and although there seemed to be considerable improvement in my walking, my left arm, chest, back and neck were very weak and entirely dependent on the plaster. I could not lift my arm at all. About two months after I came home my parents took me to see the orthopaedic surgeon who had attended me when I was in hospital. He told me that there would be no further improvement. I remember his words: "You cannot force a tired horse to climb a hill; your muscles are like old elastic." He had suggested that at some time in the future it might be possible to transfer muscles from my back to other parts but this would be a risky process and was never even considered.

By January—about twelve weeks after the original attack—I was taken out of plaster in order to try swimming. This was a great step forward, and I was enormously grateful that I was able to swim a considerable distance. I found that in the water I could use both arms. But there was still great weakness, and I was slid back into the plaster. Nevertheless, improvement was so rapid that I asked to be removed from the plaster altogether. The doctors at the hospital, including the orthopaedic surgeon I referred to, expressed surprise at my freedom of movement in view of the muscle deficiency of certain parts of my body.

The improvement continued and the muscles recovered very quickly. By March, about seven months after the attack I had 100% strength and freedom of movement throughout my body, and there was no residual impairment or wasting.

The sight difficulty that followed from the nervous breakdown and colour blindness that resulted from the illness were also healed.

This was the beginning of my interest in Christian Science and it has remained an endless source of inspiration to me.

It is often said that spiritual healing may be all very well in psychological or psychosomatic situations but not in cases of serious disease. This book directly addresses that misconception. At the same time there is a growing recognition of the seriousness of the mental health challenge in today's world, and it may be useful to include at least one example of the healing of a recognizably mental problem. The following testimony must stand as a single representative of many hundreds in a category of Christian Science healing almost as various as human nature itself.

Testimonial by Sylvia V. Lambert, then of Oswestry, Shropshire, England, published in the Christian Science Sentinel, May 12, 1980

Four years ago my husband, who is not a Christian Scientist, retired, and we set off on a four-month tour of New Zealand. The day after our return to England, I collapsed. My husband called a doctor, who had me admitted to the local mental hospital, where I stayed for two months on shock treatment and drugs.

I had been raised in Science and had attended a Christian Science Sunday School throughout my childhood. Still, despite all the advantages that could have helped me become a practicing Scientist, I allowed myself to drift from this teaching. Immersed in a very materialistic way of life, I finally concluded that church attendance was unnecessary, that it was enough to be helpful and kindly disposed toward others.

During the hospital stay, my sister, who has remained a faithful student of Science, sent me postcards on which she had written quotations from the Bible or *Science and Health with Key to the Scriptures* by Mary Baker Eddy. I promptly threw these away, until one came that said (2 Tim. 1:7), "For God hath not given us the spirit of fear; but of power, and of love, and of a sound mind." This message seemed to penetrate somewhat the veil of error within which I had cocooned myself. I slipped the card into my pocket, carried it with me everywhere, and read it many times.

My sister prayed both for my mental release and for my release from hospital. When the doctor learned that my husband had retired, he allowed me to leave the hospital. But I was given many pills to be taken daily, some for the rest of my life, and told to return to the hospital every three weeks for a checkup.

I was taken to our country cottage in the mountains, as the quiet, restful atmosphere was supposed to be an ideal aid to my recovery. But after a few weeks, instead of getting better, I seemed to be sliding backward. Then a friend, who is not a Scientist, came for the weekend. During her stay I became hysterical, and neither my husband nor she could do anything with me. Frantically my husband told her he would have to return me to the hospital.

The friend, who was acquainted with a Scientist at her office and also knew of my background, took me firmly by the arm and walked me out into the garden. Then she said, "Look, my dear, you've got to make a decision only you can make. Are you going to stay with

Christian Science, or are you going back into that hospital? Now, come on, I want an answer, now!" She has since told me that my hysterical crying stopped at once. My face, which had been grossly distorted, suddenly transformed and became serene and calm. I replied, "Why, of course, it's to be Christian Science."

We walked back into the house, where I told my husband I'd decided to rely solely on Science, and he said, "Good for you!" We then went and fetched all my pills and threw them away. Next day I rang the hospital to say that I wouldn't be keeping any more appointments with the doctor.

Instead, I made an appointment with a Christian Science practitioner. She lovingly read Mrs. Eddy's answer to the question "What is Mind?" on page 469 of *Science and Health*, which includes these words: "There can be but one Mind, because there is but one God; and if mortals claimed no other Mind and accepted no other, sin would be unknown." The sin of believing that mortal mind or brain governed me was what was pinning me to the belief of insanity. I had to understand that I was truly God's flawless child, governed by His spiritual law, which asserts its absolute supremacy over so-called material laws.

I was healed. I also realized that I'd had no desire to smoke since making the decision to depend entirely on Christian Science, even though I'd had a full cigarette case in my handbag.

My husband and I came to live permanently at our cottage in the mountains. Overflowing with gratitude, I wanted to give freely, as I had received. I joined a small Christian Science Society in a nearby town, where I was elected to serve as First Reader after only a few months membership. This position taught me a lot and had a deeply humbling effect. During this time I felt in need of class instruction so that I might learn to better apply this wonderful Science. The opportunity to receive this came during my Readership, and how helpful it was, especially when I prepared my readings for the Wednesday testimony meetings. The friend who marched me around the garden has since become interested in Christian Science. She says my healing was all the proof she needed that it really heals.

From all this I have learned that it's how *I* apply spiritual truths that matters, not what my family or fellow church members do; I am not responsible for the way anyone else interprets or utilizes Christian Science. Rather, I must make sure that the wonderful, ever-present truth that I first learned about in Sunday School, and then walked away from for so many years, is demonstrated by me every minute of every day. And what freedom this brings!

Supporting declaration of Sylvia V. Lambert in December 1982

The events related in my testimonial of healing published in the May 12, 1980, issue of the *Christian Science Sentinel*, took place in 1975. After my collapse, I was first examined by the neighborhood physician, Dr. _____, and subsequently admitted to _____ Hospital, a mental hospital in _____, England. There I was placed under the care of the head psychiatrist. I remained in the hospital for two months and on four occasions was given electro-convulsive therapy and was heavily drugged.

On my release from the hospital I was given two sets of pills with instructions for taking them three times daily. One set was for a thyroid imbalance. Until turning to Christian Science I took the prescribed drugs meticulously, though they did not produce the desired effect.

The healing has been permanent—indeed, it is as though the whole experience never happened.

Testimonial by Erna Lossow, Hamburg, Federal Republic of Germany, in the Christian Science Sentinel, November 18, 1985

[Original in German]
With great gratitude, I relate a healing that introduced me to Christian Science and gave my life spiritual direction.

When my daughter was eight years old, she became very ill. (I was divorced at the time and had sole custody of the child.) She was taken to the hospital, where she was diagnosed as having meningitis. She was immediately put in an isolation ward, and I was allowed to visit her daily but only as far as the door of her room. After she had been unconscious for days with a high fever, the chief physician informed me that my daughter would die, and that this would be for the best, since otherwise she would not be normal mentally. At that point the medical treatment was stopped.

It cannot be described how I felt. The grief settled tangibly on my mind and body like a heavy weight. On my way home that day, although I avoided people, I felt led to go and see an acquaintance who was a parish nurse. She was there, and I unburdened my heart to her. Afterward she told me that from a medical point of view there was no hope for my daughter, but that I could try Christian Science. She herself had been helped by it, she said.

I clung to this advice like a drowning person to a rope and

immediately went to the Christian Science practitioner's address she had given me. The woman who answered the door radiated love and kindness. I was with her for about two hours. Because of my bad physical and mental state, and also because Christian Science was unfamiliar to me, I did not comprehend much of what the practitioner told me. However, what I was able to take in is still as clear to me as if I had heard it yesterday. The practitioner asked me if I believed in God, and said my thinking was important, since a mother is closely connected mentally to her child. To this question I could answer "yes." Then she told me that just as a sunbeam comes from the sun, likewise man is the outcome of God, inseparable from Him. Afterward she asked if I believed that my child would be well again. Without hesitation I said, "Yes!" Even today this seems wonderful to me, because my head did not give this quick answer; it came from my heart.

The burden that had weighed so heavily on me fell away. I was free and happy. Nothing in the world could have robbed me of this joyous certainty of my daughter's healing.

When I got home, everybody thought that my daughter had died. But I said very firmly and joyously, "She will be well!" The next morning I went to the hospital. The nurse I met in the hallway told me that during the night my daughter's fever had gone and that she was now fully conscious again. When I stood at the open door, my daughter was sitting up in bed. She recognized me and smiled.

What a wonderful change had taken place in me and my daughter since I had talked with the practitioner! Even today I am grateful with all my heart for the practitioner's devoted prayer.

In about a week my daughter was released from the hospital— well, mentally and physically. In fact, some time after the healing she successfully passed an admissions examination for middle school, and her grades were better than the years before.

At the time of the healing, overcome with joy, I thought, "What a miracle!" Today I know that through the practitioner's prayerful work I had glimpsed God's love wherein is no sickness and all is perfect. *Science and Health with Key to the Scriptures* by Mary Baker Eddy states (p. 134): "There is divine authority for believing in the superiority of spiritual power over material resistance." And page 261 of the same book says: "Look away from the body into Truth and Love, the Principle of all happiness, harmony, and immortality." That was exactly what I had been led to do, and healing was the result.

Today my daughter is an active member of a branch Church of Christ, Scientist, and has two wonderful children. The Bible and the textbook, *Science and Health*, as well as other Christian Science literature, are to me the greatest guides on the road of spiritual growth. I thank and give the glory to God.

Frau Lossow and her daughter Gudrun Schlüter both furnished supporting affidavits in 1986, with details of time, place and circumstance. The mother adds that upon witnessing the daughter's "dramatic overnight recovery" the attending physician remarked, "Wir stehen vor einem Rätsel" (We stand before an enigma).

Affidavit of W. Riley Seay of Town and Country, Missouri, in August 1982

In November 1963 I received a draft notice for military service and reported to the Army Induction Center in Denver, Colorado, for a physical examination. I was just out of college and starting a business career at the time. The examination at the Induction Center was very thorough and took most of the day and included X-rays, but toward the end of the day one of the physicians there called my name and indicated that a second set of X-rays would need to be taken. When these were completed, he told me to call back the next day to learn the results. I did so and was informed that I had an active case of tuberculosis and was using one-quarter of normal lung capacity.

The Army physician to whom I spoke advised me to see a chest specialist immediately. For a number of months prior to this time I had had what I thought to be a lingering cold. I had also been experiencing night sweats, but the suggestion that I had tuberculosis came as quite a blow.

On the recommendation of a physician I knew, I consulted Dr. _____, who was at that time head of the Department of Thoracic Surgery at the University of _____ Medical School. His office was at _____ Street, _____. Dr. _____ gave me a thorough examination including not only X-rays but also skin, blood, and mucus tests, the results of which were positive and which, he informed me, showed conclusively that I had tuberculosis.

Dr. _____ broke into tears as he gave me the prognosis. He stated that I would have to stay in bed for six months to two years, that it was unlikely I would ever live a normal life again, and unlikely that I would live very long at all if I did not take bed rest right away. He recommended that I go to a sanatorium. Accordingly, I returned to my parents' home in Kingman, Kansas, with the intention of entering the Kansas Tuberculosis Sanatorium in nearby Chanute. I arrived in Kingman in late November and made an appointment in a day or so to see our family physician, Dr. A ____, whose office was at _____ Street in Kingman.

The year before I had been given a copy of the Christian Science textbook, *Science and Health with Key to the Scriptures.* I knew it had healed others and felt there must be some help for me in its 700 pages, so started reading it. My parents were not Christian Scientists and were very much opposed to my reading the textbook, however. So during the day the book stayed between the mattress and the bedspring and at night after they went to bed I would read. When I told a friend who was a Christian Scientist that I could understand very little of what I was reading, she told me to keep reading and take what I could understand. And as I continued reading the book, I found that the basis of my thought was changing.

In the meantime, I went to see Dr. _____ and had another thorough examination. He reported that the results of the skin and blood tests he administered were negative, but that the X-rays alone were enough to convince him that the condition was tuberculosis in an advanced stage. He did not prescribe medication for the condition, indicating that he wished to leave this to the physicians whose care I would be under when I entered the sanatorium. However, I returned every few days to Dr. A____ for further X-rays over the course of the next month while I was waiting for my papers to clear and for my admittance to the sanatorium. He also examined me at my home daily, since he lived next door. I was given a daily phlegm test.

I continued to read *Science and Health* at night through this period. Within a week I stopped experiencing the symptoms I'd been having—headaches, weariness, night sweats, etc. The appearance of my lungs in the X-rays taken also began to improve.

Dr. A ____ sent me in early January 1964 for an examination by another specialist, Dr. B ____ at the _____ Clinic on _____Street in _____. Dr. A ____ had sent Dr. B ____ my records, and when I arrived in his office he had all the X-rays taken of my lungs over the past month lined up on the wall. He stated that he frankly did not understand the change in the condition of my lungs. I asked him, "Are you telling me that this is not tuberculosis?" He answered that he did not know what it was. "Up here," he said (pointing to one of the early X-rays) "it is tuberculosis. Down here," (pointing to one of the latest X-rays) "it is a healthy lung." He then explained that even in cases where tuberculosis is cured there is almost always scar tissue, but that in my case there was no scar tissue whatsoever remaining on the lungs.

It wasn't long after this examination that I returned to work. I never entered the sanatorium or had any medication for the condition. Nor did I have any further lung problems. I've led an active and healthy life since then. My views of God and man were completely transformed by this experience. I went on to join the Church of Christ, Scientist and I have continued to rely on prayer in Christian Science for healing.

The final testimony in this chapter is included not merely as one more healing of tuberculosis, but because its simplicity epitomizes so much that is at the heart of Christian healing. It shows life made quietly meaningful and devoted wholly for the past twenty-eight years to helping and healing others.

Affidavit of Geraldene Harkness of Indianapolis, Indiana, in May 1983

In February of 1930, living in Terre Haute, Indiana, I became ill and very weak. I was a young bride in my early twenties. My husband took me to our family physician who was my brother-in-law, Dr. Robert Harkness. After an examination he required that I be put to bed and remain there until X-rays and further examinations could be made. Also, that my temperature be taken and recorded every four hours.

Another physician, a lung specialist, was brought in on the case. He and Dr. Harkness diagnosed the condition first as "pleurisy with effusion" and drained a large quantity of fluid from my lungs. Then came further X-rays and tests at Union Hospital in Terre Haute. Finally the condition was re-diagnosed as tuberculosis of the lungs in the early stages. The only known treatment at that time, according to the doctors, was bed rest. Therefore I was required to remain in bed twenty-four hours a day and told that this would have to continue for at least six to ten months longer. Then a decision on further steps would need to be made, based on how I was progressing.

My mother cared for me in my home. A nurse from the Prudential Life Insurance came once a week for bathing and general care plus a report to the doctors.

At this time my husband was transferred from his work in Terre Haute to Baltimore, Maryland. (This was the beginning of the Great Depression and it seemed necessary that he go where he could be sure of employment.) It was decided I should be moved to my parents' home in Indianapolis, where my mother could continue caring for me. But in the meantime, while my home was dismantled and preparations made for my move, I was cared for in the home of a registered nurse who was a friend of the family, Mrs. Amy Jones. (I must say at this point that everyone was required to keep a distance from me except the one actually caring for me. All dishes and silverware were boiled after each meal due to the fear of contagion.)

Shortly after being transferred to Mrs. Jones' home, a friend came to see me. This friend, Mrs. Elizabeth North of Terre Haute, brought with her a copy of the Christian Science textbook, *Science and Health with Key to the Scriptures.* She was not a Christian Scientist but a good Methodist. However, she said that a Christian Science friend had loaned her this little book when she was having a relationship problem and that the reading of it had given her much comfort. So she offered it to me with the thought of it giving me comfort. She didn't mention healing.

I began reading this little book out of curiosity and found that I was getting answers to questions I had wondered about since I was a child. I couldn't put the book down, I was reading every waking hour. I needed a God of Love and I was finding a God of Love. Three weeks went by like this and it was time to move me to my parents' home. I had been in bed a little over three months at this point.

In Indianapolis I was taken to the Methodist Hospital and was there for five days undergoing tests and X-rays. The doctor in charge of my case there asked that he be permitted to consult with another lung specialist for verification of his findings. We were then informed that the doctors could no longer find any trace of tuberculosis.

I shall never forget the day the lung specialist came to the foot of my bed and said, "My dear, we don't know what has happened, but we can no longer find any trace of tuberculosis." I knew then that it was the reading of that little book that had brought about the healing.

The day I was taken to the hospital in Indianapolis was in May. I remember thinking, as we were driving along, that I had never seen the sky so blue, the grass so green, or the flowers so bright as they were that day. I realized later that the regeneration taking place in consciousness at that time was all a part of the healing.

It took a little time to regain my strength after being in bed for so long, but I joined my husband in Baltimore in August of that year. In September 1931 I gave birth to a fine healthy son, although I had been told by my physician in Indianapolis that I should never have children—it would be too hard on me.

The healing was later confirmed in an unusual way. In 1941 I was a widow with a son to rear and in need of employment. I was by this time a practicing Christian Scientist. The only employment I could find, however, was in the office of Sunnyside Sanatorium, a tuberculosis sanatorium just outside of Indianapolis, Indiana. I took the position but was required to undergo a chest X-ray and physical examination before being accepted.

The examination was conducted by Dr. Jennings, Superintendent of the Sanatorium, who stated, "I see you have had tuberculosis of the lungs." He indicated that the scars from the condition were evident on the X-rays. He assured me that my case was arrested, but also informed me that the scars were permanent.

I didn't tell Dr. Jennings of my previous experience, but thought to myself that this healing isn't complete as long as there are scars. I felt sure that full healing is natural in Christian Science and would come with further spiritual regeneration. I prayed to see this more clearly realized whenever the matter would come into thought.

In subsequent years I found employment in an agency of the United States Government, the Department of Agriculture, continuing with the Government for seventeen years. During most of this time I was not required to undergo any physical examinations. However, during my last five years with the Government, I transferred to the U.S. Army Finance Center in Indianapolis, and during my last year or two with them, all employees were required to have a chest X-ray. The X-ray in my case revealed not only no tuberculosis but also no calcification or scar. I called the nurses' office to confirm this result when I received word of it.

About a year later I was listed in *The Christian Science Journal* as a full-time Christian Science practitioner.

CHAPTER 8

Personal Testament

This chapter was originally written as a letter to a Christian Scientist friend. I have retained the original form in the interest of informality and to give the reader an inside glimpse of what might otherwise be taken as mere anecdote.

Dear _____: January 1985

. . . Our doctor friend's dismissal of the testimonies of healing in our religious periodicals as "anecdotal evidence" stirs me to want to do something I should have done years ago. With all that I've written about Christian Science over the years, I've never got around to bearing witness to my own firsthand experience with this subject—not *in writing*, at any rate. So I'm going to try an experiment.

I'll try to set down in a very informal way a little of my own background in relation to Christian Science. It's first of all for your keen eye and then, if it seems to you sufficiently useful, for incorporation in the book I have now almost finished.

As you may remember, my 1958 book *Christian Science: Its Encounter with American Culture* devoted some space to the question of the evidence for Christian Science healing. But I first had to be convinced myself that the whole subject was worth treating seriously. While I was an undergraduate at Harvard in the late 1920s, I had gone through a period of healthy skepticism about Christian Science. I read all the critical material I could find on Mary Baker Eddy, *Science and Health*, the Church of Christ, Scientist, Christian Science metaphysics, Christian Science healing, etc. Some of this polemical material was extremely convincing—until I started on the research in depth which showed me how much prejudice, misunderstanding, sloppiness, and sometimes deliberate falsification of the facts lay beneath the surface of much of this critical literature.

But the one thing I could never for one moment doubt, even at my most skeptical, was the *fact* of Christian Science healing. For the simple reason that I couldn't deny what I had personally seen and experienced in my own family—who had taken up this new faith when I was ten. Before that, our family history had been one of constant illness, medication, operations, hospitalization, and precarious convalescence. After my parents became Christian Scientists everything changed totally.

The turning point was when my father, in acute agony, was told by his physician that he must be taken to the hospital immediately for an appendectomy if his life was to be saved. When the doctor left to make arrangements at the hospital, my mother—who had just begun the study of Christian Science— asked my father gently whether he really wanted to have the operation or to rely wholly on God. He gasped out "God," and she sat down beside his bed and bowed her head in prayer. I stole downstairs, greatly shaken, for in spite of all the illness we had had in the family I had never before seen such stark suffering, and my father's groans seemed to fill the house. But a few minutes later they stopped, and a period of extraordinary quiet followed. It was a quiet that seemed filled with perfect peace and assurance, a quiet within and without oneself, like nothing I had ever experienced before.

Shortly afterward my mother came downstairs and quietly said, "It's all right; he's sleeping." Within an hour, he himself emerged, perfectly free and fit, and called the hospital to cancel the appendectomy.

Was this a healing of acute appendicitis? Probably, though not certainly; a misdiagnosis is always a possibility. But something happened that day which changed all our lives. The quietness that filled our house was the revelation of a new kind of reality, of which the physical healing was only a confirmation.

From that time on, the whole household atmosphere changed radically—greatly improved health, quick healings on the few occasions when we needed them, a new spiritual strength and buoyancy, a new meaning to life.

A few years later in my mid-teens I myself had an instantaneous healing of influenza during a virulent epidemic that took a heavy toll in victims. I was staying with friends, and several of us came down with the disease the same day, but although I was completely laid out I clung to my desire not to have medical help. That day was one of the most desolating I can remember— the sort when for the first half of the day you're afraid you're going to die and for the second half you're afraid you're *not* going to die.

That evening, after my parents had been reached, I was driven home and helped up to my bedroom. My mother (who was by that time a Christian Science practitioner) spoke reassuringly to me and then prayed silently. About ten minutes later the pain, fever, inflammation, weakness—the whole miserable syndrome—simply dropped away from me in a single instant and I sprang from my bed feeling as vigorous as I'd ever felt in my life—but also with a deep sense of awe.

So even when, as an undergraduate several years (and several healings) later, I strongly doubted whether Mrs. Eddy had given the correct *explanation* of Christian Science cures, I couldn't deny the empirical *fact* of such healing. I'm speaking especially of healings I observed firsthand that one couldn't dismiss as psychosomatic—healings of close friends and some of my mother's patients, healings that in many cases had been medically diagnosed and sometimes had behind them a long history of unsuccessful medical treatment.

Incidentally, by the time I was in graduate school I was convinced that Mrs. Eddy had given the only rational explanation of these healings, lifting them out of the realm of miracle into the domain of spiritual law understood and obeyed. At the same time, study and discussions with Alfred North Whitehead and readings in the new physics had helped me to understand the distance between concrete fact and the logical abstractions constituting the "entities" of scientific theory.

Later, when I regularly read the *New England Journal of Medicine* and the *Journal of the American Medical Association* for a time as part of a research project I was working on, my convictions as to the superiority of spiritual healing were greatly strengthened, even while I learned to appreciate the dedication of the medical profession at its best. Always, however, I've sympathized with those who, not having had personal experience of Christian Science healing, look with a quizzical eye at written accounts by those who have.

I remember falling into conversation with a fellow officer in

World War II about spiritual healing. He asked for an example and I told him of my grandmother's healing in the mid-1920s of a terminal cancer. At that time she was in her sixties and lived in England, near London. A leading Harley Street specialist had informed her family that her case was beyond all hope and that all they could do was to pray that God would take her out of her suffering as quickly as possible. Her local physician reminded them of that when he told them later that she couldn't possibly last for more than a few days more.

My uncle, who was responsible for her care, had been strongly opposed to Christian Science. I remember having seen him— several years before when we were visiting the family in England—slam down the copy of *Science and Health* he had borrowed from us and burst out, "I can't waste any more time on this trash!" But with my grandmother at the very point of death, he suggested to my aunt that they call a Christian Science practitioner—not that he felt it would do the least good but simply to satisfy our branch of the family that they had taken every possible step they could. A practitioner came, sat beside my grandmother all night praying, and left in the morning. By that time a complete healing had taken place, and after two or three weeks of regaining her strength my grandmother took up her daily duties and led an active, normal, happy life for many years after.

When I told this to my Army friend, he looked at me with amazed disbelief and said, "You mean you actually *believe* that happened?" My reply in substance was that I didn't believe it; I *knew* it. If I had disbelieved it, I would have had to deny facts that were an undeniable part of my own life. I didn't expect my friend to believe it simply on my say-so or to give the same interpretation to the basic facts that I did, but for myself it was a matter of simple intellectual honesty to accept the facts as I knew them to be.

To be sure, I didn't know (or at least had forgotten by that time) the name of the Harley Street specialist and the local doctor on my grandmother's case. I didn't know the exact nature of the cancer, beyond the fact that it was internal and was in so advanced a stage that, according to the specialist, it was inoperable and untreatable by any method then known. I did know that she was in intense agony during the last months before the healing took place and that the morphine which earlier had controlled her pain was no longer effective, but I knew none of the other clinical details a medical critic would demand. However, life furnishes more supporting evidence than a set of evidential rules drawn up on the a priori assumption that such a healing is either impossible or an inexplicable freak of nature. To wit:

I stayed with my grandmother some years after her healing. She was then in her seventies, happily working for hours every day in her garden, as well as keeping her home spotless like the good Swiss housewife she had always been. At the same time I learned from my uncle how that one night's experience had changed his whole life. His former skepticism regarding Christian Science was completely reversed; he became a serious student and church member, was healed of a longstanding heart condition which had brought stern warnings from his doctors in the past, and soon he himself began to heal others.

My grandmother, on her part, never became a Christian Scientist but did go to a Wednesday evening meeting at the local Christian Science church and in the testimony period expressed her heartfelt gratitude to God for the healing she had had. Her friends and neighbors knew of the healing, of course. I knew personally the practitioner through whose prayer the healing came—a wonderful old lady who continued her healing work almost to the end of her long life. (She was almost one hundred years old when she died.)

My cousins, who were small children when the healing occurred, can't remember all the particulars, but they have been devoted Christian Scientists ever since, with a string of healings of their own; one of them has children who are also devoted Christian Scientists and who now have children of their own enrolled in the Christian Science Sunday School. So what happened during that one night of vigil and prayer by a Christian Science practitioner in my grandmother's little house in Surrey in the 1920s has had decisive effects on the lives of others down to her great-great-grandchildren in British Columbia today.

A spiritual healing, like any other religious phenomenon, is not an event isolated from all the other experiences of life—any more than a medical healing is, for that matter.

That's the problem with statistics, for all their practical utility.

They can measure only selected aspects of complex, irreducible wholes. The self-critical medical literature of recent years furnishes grim examples of new practices or remedies whose usefulness has apparently been supported by statistical evidence until a number of other broader considerations have been taken into account—the end results of side effects, faulty risk-benefit analysis, tests that produce false-positive diagnoses and lead to panicky and all-too-often fatal decisions.

I ran across an excellent summing up of some of these hazards recently in a new book by a highly reputable research scientist and clinician, a professor of medicine and physiology at Stanford University School of Medicine and consultant to the National Institutes of Health and the Veterans Administration.[1] Which leads me to a personal experience that has a direct bearing on the question of Christian Science and statistical evidence.

Back in 1957, Dr. Isabelle V. Kendig, then Chief Clinical Psychologist at the National Institute of Mental Health, was eager to make a comparative study of the health records of Christian Scientists and individuals relying on orthodox medicine. I was asked to help her in any way possible.

We explored several resources—including insurance companies, coroners' reports, and church records (the last-named notably lacking in vital statistics)—but none of them yielded the necessary information. Dr. Kendig finally got a list of a hundred men who, back in 1941–42 when they were undergraduates at [a college attended by Christian Scientists], had signed up for a special Navy program. This emergency program started their Navy training while they were still students and put them on active service as naval officers as soon as they graduated. This meant that their complete health record for several years before as well as during their active service would be on file in Washington. Dr. Kendig then drew up a control group of non-Scientist men with similar educational, social, and naval backgrounds. All that remained to be done was to get access to the official health records of both groups. Then a most unexpected and revealing problem arose.

The church authorities assured her they had no objection to the project. On the other hand, the government authorities in Washington, as soon as they heard what the project was to be, balked and refused to allow her to see the health records on which the whole study must rest. She was a respected clinical psychologist in an official position, with good connections, plenty of Washington know-how, and a perfectly reasonable request, but all this got her nowhere.

In October 1959 she wrote me: "I haven't written you sooner . . . because I've been too wretchedly frustrated. Your Church came through handsomely. I had just reached Nantucket in July when my office telephoned that Mr. Davis [Will B. Davis, at that time manager of the Christian Science Committee on Publication] had written me giving generous clearance to my project. Since then it has been held up in administrative channels here. Allegedly the only obstacle has been that your Church might not approve but I think the Public Health Service is 'leary' of anything that touches religion."

After a couple of years of unsuccessful attempts to break through this refusal to let her see the records, she gave up the effort, with some bitterness but always highly appreciative of the church's willingness to be helpful, a willingness based on the fact that the project did not in any way require an invasion of its members' privacy but would rest entirely on official government records.

Our friendship continued, and twelve years later Dr. Kendig wrote me: "As you will remember, the project I developed while I was at NIMH I could never get approved by the Government, but it might be feasible to carry it on with non-governmental resources. At least I plan to look into it. If anything should develop I shall keep you advised." A few years later she died without having found a way to carry on the research.

Our church is certainly not a statistically-minded organization, but it's interesting to me that in this case it was clearly not the church that was afraid of what the statistics might show! The reason The Mother Church has had to turn down almost all the research projects suggested to it by sociologists and academic investigators of various sorts is the built-in impracticality of their proposals. The church simply doesn't have the information or statistics asked for and refuses to bombard its members with elaborate questionnaires prying into every aspect of their private lives, bodily conditions, physical activities, personal life-styles, family histories of disease, etc.

Such an attitude in an age of computerized data banks and instant information retrieval systems is of course regarded generally as rankest heresy. On the other hand, the names and locations of all the testifiers whose accounts are published in the Christian Science periodicals are always printed along with the testimony, so anyone who wants to is free to investigate further via the individual or individuals concerned.

At times, as in the case of my grandmother's healing, further details are impossible to pick up at this late date, so if I decide to include this letter in my book the reader will have to decide for himself or herself whether I am an unconscionable liar, a neurotic fantasist, a gullible stooge, or a number of other possibilities, including the possibility of my being an honest and responsible writer! I have faith that on such matters an accurate assessment *can* be made by an honest and responsible reader.

At any rate I'm going to include one final incident from my family history to round off these comments. The incident took place at least thirty years ago. I have no idea how I could get supporting evidence today. But some of the details are as vivid to me now as when my mother told me of the experience the day after it happened—with the weather still near zero, the streets still icy, and her face lighted up with quiet gratitude.

First, a little background.

When she and my father became engaged, her physician warned him not to expect her to live beyond the age of forty at the most, adding in the casual way of doctors at the turn of the century that she didn't have "a sound organ in her body." Actually, soon after reaching forty she was rescued from her semi-invalidism by Christian Science and spent most of the next forty years of her life bringing healing, comfort, moral courage, transformation of character and circumstance to scores of people who turned to her as a Christian Science practitioner.

On this particular occasion, when she was in her late seventies, she had a call about two a.m. from a nurse at Harvard's Stillman Infirmary, asking her whether she could go there immediately for an emergency case. She was living alone in her Cambridge apartment, but consented, dressed quickly, ventured out on the icy and empty streets (the temperature close to zero), found a taxi at a nearby hotel and was at the infirmary within an hour.

The patient, she found, was a man who was not expected to live through the night but had expressed a sudden wish to have help from a Christian Science practitioner as a last resort. My mother often had Harvard and M.I.T. students come to her for help, and he may have heard her name from one of them. At any rate, she was led to his bedside by the nurse who had called her and who was obviously full of curiosity; then she sat down beside the patient, talked to him a little, and prayed a great deal. By seven or eight in the morning the man was completely healed.

When the stunned doctor on the case had made sure of this, he asked my mother whether she would be willing to stay awhile longer to talk with him (the doctor). She agreed, and for almost an hour he plied her with questions about what she was doing mentally while she sat beside the patient. She explained that prayer in Christian Science is not a human mind process or a form of suggestion, but a humble and wholehearted turning to God and a listening for His voice. I can't pretend to know all that she said to him; but knowing her, I'm sure of one thing— whatever she said was filled with her deep, lifelong love of the Bible, especially of Christ Jesus as the Son of God and son of man—the "life-link" between divinity and humanity—and filled, too, with the unselfed compassion and inner joy that always marked her Christianity.

One learns vastly more from lives than from arguments. And most of all from one's own experiences in the healing work. I don't know of any greater joy than seeing a patient lifted up from suffering or despair through one's reaching out in prayer to grasp the spiritual fact behind the material appearance. . . .

R. P.

Postscript

In the opening chorus of his verse drama *The Rock*, T. S. Eliot deplores the age's "Knowledge of words, and ignorance of the Word," then asks:

> Where is the Life we have lost in living?
> Where is the wisdom we have lost in knowledge?
> Where is the knowledge we have lost in information?[1]

Eliot wrote those lines some fifty years ago, but their elegiac quality has a sharper edge today. In the early thirties religion was backing away awkwardly before the mounting claims of politics, economics, and the totalitarian nightmare. Today even one's innermost religious convictions are expected to genuflect before the demands of technocratic imperialism, information systems aimed at achieving mechanized omniscience, computerized psychology, biomedical authority, and world salvation by "mutual assured destruction" (MAD).

These issues raise again the underlying question of qualitative values versus quantitative measurements. Is a life, for instance, to be judged by the years it lasts or the values it embodies? In human terms, both are important, but so is Eliot's question: "Where is the Life we have lost in living?" Is a human life enriched by several additional years of vegetable existence? Is that the sort of thing Jesus meant by his words: "I am come that they might have life, and that they might have it more abundantly" (John 10:10)? Or what Mrs. Eddy meant by her last written words in her ninetieth year: "God is my life"?[2]

The concerns of even the most ardent proponent of Christian

healing go far beyond the cure of disease. I think back to my own lifelong concern with public affairs and social action, peace and war, science and art, scholarship and journalism, people and ideas. These are not rivals of spiritual healing; they are demands for its extension to all that would keep the human spirit enslaved by material process.

Christian Science claims to have something extremely valuable to contribute to the "healing" of these larger issues. Yet it can do so only to the extent that it demonstrates in unmistakable ways the actuality of Spirit, or what Mrs. Eddy called "the superiority of spiritual power over material resistance."[3]

This is where the importance of tangible, demonstrable Christian healing, as practiced by Jesus, is crucial. Yet now, as in his day, it is not the purpose of such healing merely to make people "comfortable in matter." As *Science and Health* puts it: "Now, as then, signs and wonders are wrought in the metaphysical healing of physical disease; but these signs are only to demonstrate its divine origin,—to attest the reality of the higher mission of the Christ-power to take away the sins of the world."[4]

To be satisfied with the mere achievement of physical well-being and a smooth middle-class life style is in itself a sin in a world overwhelmingly in need of the healing of its social as well as its personal ills. Mrs. Eddy had words quite as hard as the Hebrew prophets' for those of her followers who thought they were taking off on a joy ride to heaven. The "song" of Christian Science, she once wrote to her church in Boston, was: "Work—work—work—watch and pray."[5]

Many practitioners report that while some of their most medically serious cases have yielded quickly and easily to their spiritual treatment, others much less dangerous but involving deep-rooted mental and moral factors have sometimes required prolonged work, study, struggle, persistence, and patient love—on both the practitioner's and the patient's parts—before the healing came.

This is the dimension of Christian Science almost absent from the accounts of healing chosen for this book. Focusing on the interface between medicine and a healing method that relies wholly on prayer has required the emphasis to be on the factual evidence demanded in today's world. As a result, physical and medical details have been stressed at the expense of far more important spiritual and theological concerns.

For the same reason, many of the accounts in this book include a detailing of bodily symptoms that would not be permitted in testimonies published in the Christian Science periodicals, which avoid giving vivid pictures of disease. The normal purposes of such testimonies are to bear witness to the goodness of God, express gratitude for blessings received, and give moral encouragement to readers who may be seeking a healing. They are not aimed at convincing determined materialists!

This would probably be true of Christian healers in any denomination who follow the spirit of Paul's injunction: "Whatsoever ye do, do all to the glory of God" (1 Cor. 10:31). The desire to glorify God by healing humanity may be the almost invisible bond that unites even the dedicated Christian physician or surgeon with the Christian Scientist.

In a different way, the natural scientist and the Christian Scientist are linked, however remotely, by a common repudiation of "miracles" as infractions of universal law. Both also recognize that all scientific truth must be validated in actual experience.

This last point, however, is the very thing that has seemed to Mrs. Eddy's critics most scandalous in her teachings. For instance, it is possible for both the theologian and the scientist to tolerate philosophical idealists who argue for the unreality of matter. This can be accommodated as ingenious speculation even when rejected as factual absurdity. But to have a nineteenth-century woman with no philosophic credentials present the proposition as something with radical practical consequences—something capable of healing a terminal cancer, for example—was clearly outrageous in her own day and is still an offense in ours.

Yet this is the century in which relativity and quantum theory have opened the door a crack to the possibility of a different *order* of being, a different *kind* of reality. Twentieth-century physics suggests reality may be different from that posited by the reductionist, determinist, or "scientific" materialism of the past— and posited still by the biomedical hardliner of today.

This is the century in which a Heisenberg could insist that the "common division of the world into subject and object, inner world and outer world, body and soul is no longer adequate"[6]; in which (to recall two core statements already quoted) a Pauli could concede the possibility of further scientific developments that will "move towards a unitary world-view in which science is only a part in the whole," and a Schrödinger could warn that science must "be prepared to find a new type of physical law"—more properly of "nonphysical" or "super-physical" law—prevailing in the world.[7]

This is the century in which many philosophers and scientists can write almost casually that "from the standpoint of philosophy the distinction between the physical and mental is superficial and unreal"[8]; that to "assert that there is *only* matter and no mind is the most illogical of propositions, quite apart from the findings of modern physics . . . that there is no matter in the traditional meaning of the term[9]; that matter and substance are "mathematical abstractions" and "mind and body are one"[10]; that we "can never speak about nature without, at the same time, speaking about ourselves"[11]; that the central change required by quantum and relativity theory has been the "dropping of the notion of analysis of the world into relatively autonomous parts, separately existent but in interaction" and as a result "the primary emphasis is now on *undivided wholeness,* in which the observing instrument is not separated from what is observed."[12]

Yet matter—as "a practical matter"—still remains the starting point of most human thinking. Theoretically, to be sure, biblical theology starts with God. "In the beginning God. . . . " (Gen. 1:1). "In the beginning was the Word, and the Word was with God, and the Word was God" (John 1:1), or, in the clarifying words of the New English Bible, "what God was, the Word was." But practically speaking, the crucial Christian faith that "the Word was made flesh and dwelt among us" has led most theologians to be quite as eager as any microbiologist to hang on to the substantiality of matter, regardless of the logical implications of the new physics.

Christian Science advances on the problem in a different way:

"The Word was made flesh." Divine Truth must be known by its effects on the body as well as on the mind, before the Science of being can be demonstrated. Hence its embodiment in the incarnate

Jesus,—that life-link forming the connection through which the real reaches the unreal, Soul rebukes sense, and Truth destroys error.[13]

Christian healing is possibly the point at which the supremacy of matter is most directly challenged. Even in the modified form in which doctor and pastor team up to supplement technology with prayer, two different sorts of universe are implied though not acknowledged. Beautiful results may sometimes follow from cooperation with a doctor who himself believes deeply in Christian prayer, but a central ambiguity remains a permanent weakness in such as undertaking. Pragmatically the two approaches may work; logically they represent incompatible theories of cause and effect.

Obviously a democratic society requires pragmatic adjustments as well as mutual tolerance between disparate systems. But a technological culture that tries to eliminate other value systems without any serious effort to understand them—either as a way of thinking or as a way of life—is depriving itself of an invaluable challenge to its own unquestioned assumptions. History surely makes one thing crystal clear: that the dominant presuppositions of any age and culture will change radically with the passing of time. A civilization worthy of the name must be willing to doubt its certainties as well as its priorities.

Then where on earth can certainty be found?

A Christian might well answer, "In the divine love and power revealed and exemplified in Jesus Christ." But that can be true only if Christians are able to demonstrate in their own lives the ever-presence of that supreme love and the universality of that redeeming power. Jesus said simply, "He that believeth on me, the works that I do shall he do also," adding the promise that when he was no longer with his followers in person they should achieve "greater works" (John 14:12).

Christian healing—which has reappeared surprisingly in an age that somewhat prematurely prides itself on its mastery of nature—may still be in its babe-in-the-manger stage. But if the analogy holds, this new advent will not be easily ignored. Looking back on the earlier appearing and the earthshaking changes that followed the spread of primitive Christianity, Yeats could write with a flash of audacious paradox:

The Roman Empire stood appalled:
It dropped the reins of peace and war
When that fierce virgin and her Star
Out of the fabulous darkness called.[14]

Once more we are in a time of earthshaking change—of fabulous darkness, doomsday threats, star wars, collapsing values. But also a time of shining spiritual promise and new beginnings. A time to look into overlooked mangers and follow unscheduled stars for fresh evidence of the revolutionary power of Spirit in human affairs.

A time, also, for healing old misunderstandings.

Notes

PREFACE

1. Robert Inchausti, "Solzhenitsyn: Postmodern Moralist," *The Christian Century,* November 14, 1984, p. 1066: "He tells the stories of hundreds of lives in order to bring home in a way that outstrips any ideological explanation the complete meaning of what has taken place."
2. Geoffrey Hoyland, *The Resurrection Pattern* (London: Duckworth, 1947), p. 52. Hoyland's emphasis.

CHAPTER 1: A HARD LOOK AT AN ODD COSMOS

1. Robert E. Egner and Lester E. Dennon, eds., *Basic Writings of Bertrand Russell* (New York: Simon & Schuster, 1961), pp. 67, 72.
2. Steven Weinberg, *The First Three Minutes* (New York: Basic Books, 1977), p. 144.
3. George Santayana, *Interpretations of Poetry and Religion* (New York: Scribner, 1911), p. 228.

CHAPTER 2: A TRAVELER FROM INNER SPACE

1. Mary Burt Messer, *The Science of Society* (New York: Philosophical Library, 1959), p. 7.
2. Howard Clark Kee, *Miracle in the Early Christian World* (New Haven: Yale University Press, 1983). Kee says of later Bultmannians: "The initial assumption is that the real Jesus could not have done such an intellectually embarrassing thing as performing miracles" (p. 292).
3. Paul Tillich, *The New Being* (New York: Scribner, 1955), p. 42. Cf. Raymond E. Brown, *New Testament Essays* (New York: Paulist Press, 1982), p. 171: "The miracle was not primarily an external guarantee of the coming of the kingdom; it was one of the means by which the kingdom came." Also Michael Grant, *Jesus: An Historian's Review of the Gospels* (New York: Scribner, 1977), p. 34: "Thus the medically curative and philanthropic aspects of Jesus' healings were

secondary to his main intention, which was to signify that the Reign of God had begun. . . . Jesus' cures . . . were not only symbolic seals of his mission but at the same time actual victories in the battle that had already been joined against the forces of evil."

4. Quoted in Robert Peel, *Christian Science: Its Encounter with American Culture* (New York: Holt, 1958), p. 193 n. 16.

5. Evelyn Frost, *Christian Healing* (London: Mowbrae & Co., 1954); Morton Kelsey, *Healing and Christianity* (New York: Harper & Row, 1975).

6. Augustine, *The City of God*, trans. Gerald G. Walsh and Daniel J. Honan (New York: Fathers of the Church, 1954), p. 445.

7. Dr. Rex Gardner, "Miracles of Healing in Anglo-Celtic Northumbria as Recorded by the Venerable Bede and His Contemporaries: A Reappraisal in the Light of Twentieth-Century Experience," *British Medical Journal* (Dec. 24–31, 1983), pp. 1927–33.

8. Ibid., p. 1927.

9. Ernst and Marie-Luise Keller, *Miracles in Dispute: A Continuing Debate* (London: SCM Press, 1969), p. 227: "Scholars are generally agreed that Jesus healed the sick. . . . Of course we do not think today that all the miracles of healing reported in the New Testament really took place in reality exactly as they are reported to have done. . . . But we cannot in general deny the possibility that Christian faith, from which a liberating influence radiated, also led to liberation from physical ills in certain predisposed cases. What was here possible or impossible can hardly be decided in detail as long as psychosomatic medicine is still in its infancy and as long as the interrelations of the mental and spiritual with the physical being are still insufficiently clarified."

10. This and the next four quotations are from Beard's account as quoted in A. Graham Ikin, *New Concepts of Healing* (New York: Association Press, 1956), pp. 104–8.

11. For a summary of the evidence available today, see Robert Peel, *Mary Baker Eddy: The Years of Discovery* (New York: Holt, Rinehart & Winston, 1966), pp. 195–97 and 344–46 nn. 1–21. Also *Mary Baker Eddy: The Years of Authority* (New York: Holt, Rinehart & Winston, 1977), p. 231.

12. Mary Baker Eddy, *Miscellaneous Writings* (Boston: The First Church of Christ, Scientist, 1924), p. 24.

13. Eddy, *Science and Health*, p. 109.

14. Ibid., p. ix.

CHAPTER 3: HEALING THE SICK: SCIENCE OR ART?

1. Mary Baker Eddy, *Retrospection and Introspection* (Boston: The First Church of Christ, Scientist, 1920), p. 94. For the "modesty" of Jesus, see Matt. 11:29; 19:16, 17; Luke 22:27; John 5:19, 30; 13:1–16; 14:12, 28; 20:17.

2. See Stephen Toulmin, *The Return to Cosmology* (Berkeley and Los Angeles: University of California Press, 1982), p. 46.

3. See Lewis Thomas, *The Youngest Science* (New York: Viking, 1984).

4. Ivan Illich, *Medical Nemesis* (New York: Pantheon Books, 1976); Robert S. Mendelsohn, *Confessions of a Medical Heretic* (Chicago: Contemporary Books, 1979).

5. Derek Bok, "Needed: A New Way to Train Doctors," President's Report to the Harvard Board of Overseers, 1982–83, *Harvard Magazine* (May–June 1984), p. 41.

6. Eddy, *Science and Health with Key to the Scriptures* (Boston: The First Church of Christ, Scientist, 1934), p. 164.

7. Eddy, *Miscellaneous Writings* (Boston: The First Church of Christ, Scientist, 1924), p. 19.

8. Dava Sobel, "The Hospital Fever," *Harvard Magazine* (May–June 1978), p. 30.

9. D. E. Harken, "The Future of Cardiac Surgery," in *Cardiac Surgery*, ed. John C. Norman (New York: Appleton, Century, Crofts, 1972), p. 689.

10. Bok, "Needed," p. 39.

11. Quoted in Richard A. Knox, "Surgery or Not?" *Boston Globe*, Aug. 15, 1984, p. 2.

12. Bok, "Needed," p. 38.

13. René Dubos, *Mirage of Health* (New York: Harper & Bros., 1959), pp. 17, 234.

14. Erwin Schrödinger, *What Is Life?* (Cambridge: Cambridge University Press, 1946), p. 86.

15. Werner Heisenberg, *Physics and Beyond* (New York: Harper & Row, 1971), p. 215.

16. This occurred after a noonday testimony meeting at Fifth Church of Christ, Scientist, New York, in 1953 or 1954. The man who spoke to Einstein was George Nay, a Christian Science lecturer, originally from Hungary, later an editor of the various foreign-language editions of *The Christian Science Herald*. His account of this brief encounter with Einstein is on file in the Archives of The First Church of Christ, Scientist, in Boston, but I have also heard it directly from Nay himself.

17. Quoted in Arthur Koestler, *The Roots of Coincidence* (London: Hutchinson, 1972), p. 90. Emphasis added.

18. Cf. such venturesome theorists as physicists Fritjof Capra poking into the "biomedical model" (*The Turning Point* [New York: Simon & Schuster, 1982]) and Fred Alan Wolf looking over the neurosciences (*Star Wave: Mind, Consciousness, and Quantum Physics* [New York: Macmillan, 1984]). For a simply expressed overview of the revolution in progress see Robert M. Augrus and George N. Stanciu, *The New Story of Science* (Lake Bluff, IL: Regnery Gateway, 1984).

19. Eddy, *Science and Health*, p. 571.

20. David Hilfiker, "Facing Our Mistakes," *New England Journal of Medicine* (Jan. 12, 1984), pp. 118–22.

21. Eddy, *Science and Health*, p. 444.

CHAPTER 4: FAITH AND WORKS IN A PLURALISTIC SOCIETY

1. Mary Baker Eddy, *Science and Health with Key to the Scriptures* (Boston: The First Church of Christ, Scientist, 1934), p. 1.

2. Eddy, *Rudimental Divine Science* (Boston: The First Church of Christ, Scientist, 1936), p. 2.

3. *A Century of Christian Science Healing* (Boston: Christian Science Publishing Society, 1966), p. 248.

4. Alexander Roberts and James Donaldson, eds., *The Ante-Nicene Fathers*, vol. 2 (New York: Scribner, 1926), p. 73.

5. Geoffrey Hoyland, *The Resurrection Pattern* (London: Duckworth, 1947), p. 67.

6. Eddy, *Miscellaneous Writings* (Boston: The First Church of Christ, Scientist, 1924), p. 365.

7. Eddy, *Science and Health*, p. 313.

8. *A Century of Christian Science Healing*, pp. 239–41.

9. Thomas Johnsen, "Christian Scientists and the Medical Profession: A Historical Perspective," *Medical Heritage* 2, No. 1 (Jan./Feb. 1986), pp. 70–78.

10. *A Century of Christian Science Healing,* p. 241.
11. Eddy, *Manual of The Mother Church* (Boston: The First Church of Christ, Scientist, 1936), p. 48.
12. See Eddy, *Science and Health,* pp. 443–44.
13. This statement has been challenged by some members of the Massachusetts Department of Public Health. However, it is supported by a press statement issued by Dr. Nicholas J. Fiumara, the department's Director of the Division of Communicable Diseases, on October 28, 1972, to correct some misleading newspaper stories about the church's position on immunization: "In order to correct any misconception in newspaper stories it should be pointed out that Christian Scientists are indeed fully cooperating with my office. However, since we already have 95% immunization in this State there is no need for total immunization. If there were need for more I would have ordered it and Christian Scientists would have cooperated as they have for the past thirty years I have worked with them." Where problems have arisen in regard to immunization, quarantine, the reporting of suspected contagious diseases, or other causes, this has almost always resulted from church members' ignorance or disregard of church policies in regard to such matters. In two highly publicized instances where epidemics have hit schools catering to Christian Scientists, insufficient attention to such policies and delay in communicating with those responsible for implementing them has made cooperation with public health authorities less prompt and effective than has normally been the case in Christian Science history.
14. Eddy, *Science and Health,* p. 15.
15. William James, letter to the *Boston Transcript* (1894), quoted in Robert Peel, *Christian Science: Its Encounter with American Culture* (New York: Holt, 1958), p. 137.

CHAPTER 5: TEST AND TESTIMONY

1. Eddy memorandum in Archives of The Mother Church. Quoted in Robert Peel, *Mary Baker Eddy: The Years of Authority* (New York: Holt, Rinehart & Winston, 1977), p. 223.
2. *The American Journal of Sociology,* March 1954, pp. 448–53, and September 1954, pp. 184–85.
3. *A Century of Christian Science Healing* (Boston: Christian Science Publishing Society, 1966), p. 160.
4. Allison W. Phinney, Jr., "The Spirituality of Mankind," *Christian Science Sentinel,* Sept. 3, 1984, pp. 1529–33.

NOTES TO "THE SPIRITUALITY OF MANKIND," PP. 50–53.

1. Clifford P. Smith, *Christian Science and Legislation* (Boston: Christian Science Publishing Society, 1909), p. 109.
2. Ibid., p. 113.
3. Eddy, *Message to the Mother Church for 1900* (Boston: The First Church of Christ, Scientist, 1900), p. 10.
4. Eddy, *Miscellaneous Writings* (Boston: The First Church of Christ, Scientist, 1924), p. 245.
5. John 16:33.

CHAPTER 6: DEMONSTRATION AND ACCUSATION

1. Christian Science Committee on Publication files.
2. *A Century of Christian Science Healing* (Boston: Christian Science Publishing Society, 1966), p. 240.
3. Mary Baker Eddy, *Science and Health*, pp. 167, 443.
4. Mark Twain, *Christian Science* (New York: Harper, 1907), p. 60.
5. Eddy, *Science and Health*, p. 130.

CHAPTER 7: A CLOUD OF WITNESSES

1. Robert Peel, "The Christian Science Practitioner," in *Journal of Pastoral Counseling* 4, 1 (Spring 1969): p. 40.

CHAPTER 8: PERSONAL TESTAMENT

1. Eugene D. Robin, M.D., *Matters of Life and Death: Risks vs. Benefits of Medical Care* (New York: W. H. Freeman, 1984).

POSTSCRIPT

1. T. S. Eliot, *Collected Poems 1909–1935* (New York: Harcourt, Brace, 1936), p. 179.
2. Robert Peel, *Mary Baker Eddy: The Years of Authority* (New York: Holt, Rinehart & Winston, 1977), p. 359.
3. Mary Baker Eddy, *Science and Health with Key to the Scriptures*, p. 134.
4. Ibid., p. 150.
5. Eddy, *Message for 1900* (Boston: The First Church of Christ, Scientist, 1900), p. 2.
6. Quoted in Paul Davies, *God and the New Physics* (New York: Simon & Schuster, 1983), p. 112.
7. See pp. 27, 29.
8. Bertrand Russell, *The Analysis of Matter* (London: Allen & Unwin, 1954), p. 402.
9. Valdemar A. Firsoff, *Life, Mind, and Galaxies* (Edinburgh: Oliver & Boyd, 1967), p. 52.
10. Roger S. Jones, *Physics as Metaphor* (New York: New American Library, 1982), p. 140.
11. Fritjov Capra, *The Turning Point* (New York: Simon & Schuster, 1982), p. 87.
12. David Bohm, *Wholeness and the Implicate Order* (London: Routledge & Kegan Paul, 1980), p. 134.
13. Eddy, *Science and Health*, p. 350.
14. William Butler Yeats, "Two Songs from a Play," in *Collected Poems* (New York: Macmillan, 1951), p. 210.